Book Clubbing!

Book Clubbing!

Successful Book Clubs for Young People

Carol Littlejohn

 LINWORTH

AN IMPRINT OF ABC-CLIO, LLC
Santa Barbara, California • Denver, Colorado • Oxford, England

Library of Congress Cataloging-in-Publication Data

Littlejohn, Carol.
 Book clubbing! : successful book clubs for young people / Carol Littlejohn.
 p. cm.
 Includes bibliographical references and index.
 ISBN 978-1-58683-414-2 (hard copy : alk. paper) — ISBN 978-1-58683-415-9
(ebook) 1. Group reading. I. Title.

 LC6631.L58   2011
 028—dc22   2010053242

ISBN: 978-1-58683-414-2
EISBN: 978-1-58683-415-9

15 14 13 12 11   1 2 3 4 5

This book is also available on the World Wide Web as an eBook.
Visit www.abc-clio.com for details.

Linworth
An Imprint of ABC-CLIO, LLC

ABC-CLIO, LLC
130 Cremona Drive, P.O. Box 1911
Santa Barbara, California 93116-1911

This book is printed on acid-free paper ∞

Manufactured in the United States of America

This book is dedicated to all "my" book clubbers, especially
Sarah Bastone, Michael Mann, and Marissa Helides.

As always, a special thanks to my sons, Karl and Drew.

Thanks, Cathlyn Thomas, for proofreading this
book and adding many helpful suggestions.

Thanks, too, to the team at Linworth Publishing,
especially my inspiring editor, Cyndee Anderson.

Finally, this book is dedicated to my parents,
Dr. Frank Thomas (1921–2008) and Mary Veach Thomas (1921–1997).

Contents

About the Author

CAROL LITTLEJOHN is coauthor (with Cathlyn Thomas) of the *Talk That Book* series, vols. 1–4 (Worthington, OH: Linworth, 1998–2004). Her 20-year experience as a public and school librarian has taken her from Pittsburgh, Pennsylvania, to Johannesburg, South Africa. Check out her reading Web site at www.carollittlejohn.com.

Reading Activities Matrix

All ages can participate in these suggested reading activities. However, this matrix recommends the most successful activities by grade. For further information on each activity, see chapter 5, "Reading Activities: The Fun Begins."

	Pre–K	Kdg.	Gr. 1–3	Gr. 4–6	Gr. 7–9	Gr. 10+
Arts and Crafts	X	X	X	X	X	X
Authors, Authors!		X	X	X	X	X
Battle of the Books				X	X	X
Book Exchange			X	X	X	X
Book Trailers			X	X	X	X
Creative Dramatics	X	X	X	X	X	X
Field Trips	X	X	X	X	X	X
Guest Speakers	X	X	X	X	X	X
Mystery Games		X	X	X	X	X
One-Minute Booktalks	X	X	X	X	X	X
Poster Contest	X	X	X	X	X	X
Puppet Show				X	X	X
Rapping Rhymes	X	X	X	X	X	X
Read-Aloud Books	X	X	X			
Reader's Theater				X	X	X
Reading Games	X	X	X	X		
ScrapBooking			X	X	X	X
Soap Opera					X	X
Storytelling	X	X	X	X	X	X
Talent Show	X	X	X	X	X	X
Trial by Jury			X	X	X	X
Young Authors and Illustrators	X	X	X	X	X	X

Introduction

Why book clubbing? How is a youth book club different from an adult book club? Can book clubs create lifelong readers?

This book is different from most books on book clubs. Instead of focusing on a group-read (a group reading one selected book), I address other successful methods of running a book club. These methods come from my experiences, as well as those of other adult sponsors who lead book clubs that give students reading choices with fun reading activities.

I began sponsoring a book club in 2000 with two Reading teachers, Deborah Beresik and Desiree Rotundo. Our middle school (grades 6–8) was located outside Pittsburgh, Pennsylvania. We sponsored young adults, ages 11–14, for 45 minutes weekly during an Activity Period. Our group had about 30 students with a wide variety of reading skills and interests. At first we tried Reader's Theater—a triumph. Next we resorted to the tried-and-true group-read—not so successful. The group's interest dwindled until we all agreed on another reading activity.

After this experience, choice became a vital ingredient in all the activities we did. Thereafter, each book club morphed into a self-sufficient unit led by the students, and our job was to initiate their democratic wishes: field trips, mystery games, guest speakers, shared booktalks, and storytelling.

Success! Two years later, I had to divide the book club into three groups because of expanding membership, but we came together for our annual field trip. As different and varied as each of the groups became, all members wanted activities to accompany each meeting. That was an aha moment. Could a book club be that flexible?

As I discovered, a flexible book club requires a multitude of reading activities. Preceding this introduction is a Reading Activities Matrix that provides suggested activities for each grade. More specific details are provided in chapter 5. Reading activities usually occur at the end of the meeting. However, a successful book club requires more than just fun reading activities.

Chapter 1, "Just the Facts," provides research on reading by educators like Harvey Daniels and Stephen Krashen that encourages more choice in reading. Valuable reading research has been studied and analyzed since 1937, and we can apply the successful strategies these studies suggest.

Chapter 2, "Back to Our (Book) Sponsors," discusses the adult leaders, or what I call sponsors. It helps to know the latest research, but I think the real experts are the sponsors. Generally, sponsors don't conduct research studies or write articles, and yet their ideas are usually practical and reliable. This chapter gives practical tips and advice from the sponsors based on their practical experiences.

Chapter 3, "Make It Work! The Place Setting," analyzes the environmental setting. Where is the book club? Is the setting private or open? Can the members bring their lunch or snacks to the setting? What media, if any, are available? The setting has so much to do with the activities. Whatever the setting, the sponsor must make the space work.

Chapter 4, "The Book Clubbers: Let's Go Clubbing!," deals with the participants, or what I call the book clubbers. They are the main ingredients of a successful book club. In this chapter, book clubbers give helpful opinions. What did they like about the book club? What did they dislike? This chapter also discusses using a *Reader's Profile* for preteens and teens that is distributed at the first meeting. These anonymous profiles are collected by the sponsor and analyzed with the group at the next meeting. From the second meeting, the book club takes its direction from the students.

As noted earlier, chapter 5, "Reading Activities: The Fun Begins," provides you with an alphabetical listing of reading activities for all ages.

Chapter 6, "Cover to Cover: Recommended Group-Reads," provides suggestions for a *group-read*, in which one book is selected for a group. Although we never tried a group-read again, I think that these titles might have worked, especially if your book club has a specific age, gender, or theme.

Chapter 7, "Talk That Book! Book Club Resources," deals with media that recommend books for book clubs, including books, magazines, and Web sites.

The Appendices contain reproducible forms: "Battle of the Books" Timeline, Book Club Permission Slip, Guest Speaker Checklist, Permission Form for Field Trips, Publishing Permission Form, and Reader's Profile.

Readers should feel free to browse and select the appropriate activities. Sometimes I refer the reader to a chapter because I'm assuming that the reader has not read the book chronologically. Therefore, please excuse any redundancy.

Finally, I hope this book will begin a discussion on engaging all kinds of readers in book clubs. Book clubs should include all readers, including students that are

✦ Learning English as a second language

✦ Attending special education classes

✦ Avoiding leisure reading

A group-read may not appeal to these reluctant readers because of the environmental similarity to a classroom. Instead, if the group democratically decides on its own book selection and reading activities, members are participating in student-led activities that may have long-term results.

I would enjoy hearing any ideas or suggestions from other book club sponsors (librarians, teachers, parents, and volunteers). I would also like to hear from book clubbers. Please share your ideas and experiences with me on my Web site. Also, for your convenience, I will put most of the Web sites I mention in this book on my Web site, including any updates.

In the meantime, let's go book clubbing!

Carol Littlejohn
www.carollittlejohn.com

CHAPTER 1

Just the Facts:
Research on Reading
and Book Clubs

Most educators don't have time to read the latest research on reading. However, if you know some of the facts, you can implement some proven results into your book club.

+ **Choice** plays a vital role in encouraging children to read. Choice includes allowing the reader to select the environment, reading material, and activity.

+ **Leisure reading declines among preteens** because of certain behaviors: watching television or video games, participating in other activities, and avoiding reading because of lack of skills or interest.

+ **Extrinsic rewards are not beneficial in encouraging lifelong reading.** Avid readers hate the reading-rewards programs more than reluctant readers. All students want to choose their books and don't like being told what to read.

+ **Reluctant readers prefer graphic novels, magazines, and books in series.** Avid readers also like these reading materials, but they read more diverse materials and select reading over television.

+ **Low-income readers do not have the same access to materials as do middle- and high-income readers.** This puts them at a disadvantage that needs to be addressed by the book club sponsor.

+ **Reading is on the rise in all categories and ages**, according to a 2009 study by the National Endowment for the Arts.

Let's address each component separately.

Choice. Ironically, while researchers know how vital choice is to encourage reading, educators insist on selecting the books that young people read. Isn't this self-defeating? Instead, what about sponsoring a student-led book club that gives the young people choice in their reading selections?

For example, the Oprah Book Club sparked a reading revolution for adults. However, when Oprah Winfrey began the Oprah Book Club, Jr. for young people, this program did not have the same success. Although *School Library Journal* reported the lack of enthusiasm for the new program, the writer did not offer an opinion why the program failed to ignite the same enthusiasm (Margolis). Perhaps selecting one book to read does not offer young people choice in their reading. Young people read at a variety of reading levels, and one book may not appeal to a wide range of ages (Littlejohn "Oprah Revolution" 28–29).

By reading, students improve their reading and writing skills, including spelling and vocabulary (Krashen 3). Should educators be concerned if the reading material is on a reading list? What about students who read comic or picture books? Are they to be excluded?

According to multiple reading studies, readers will select a harder reading level if the subject interests them (Krashen 87–89; Littlejohn "Why" 2; McKool; Miller; Smoldt 10). Perhaps one way to encourage leisure reading is to discover a student's interests and then provide related material. Once again, this approach individualizes a student's reading interests over a group-read.

Leisure reading. "If promoting voluntary reading is a goal of parents and teachers, then it appears that introducing and encouraging the reading of these kind of materials (series books, graphic novels, magazines) in balance with the more conventional literature, is critical" (McKool).

If your purpose is to encourage leisure reading, consider allowing readers to read whatever interests them. If these readers want to share their reading with others, certainly they will have the chance. Many will become experts in booktalking and lead others in discovering their books. Peer recommendations are always powerful. Others will choose not to share their reading experiences, and that's fine, too. By sponsoring a book club, you demonstrate that leisure reading is as important as other school activities.

Extrinsic rewards. This controversial topic of rewarding readers through prizes or awards is still being debated. However, most researchers agree that rewarding readers has minimal long-term results, especially in developing lifelong readers. McKool emphatically states that avid readers hate the reading-rewards programs more than reluctant readers do. Once again, students want to choose their reading material, including graphic novels (Krashen 109–110; McKool; Littlejohn "Why" 2; Miller and Ogranovitch; Zemelman et al.).

Reluctant readers. Reluctant readers do not enjoy leisure reading. Sometimes these reluctant readers lack reading skills or confidence. Maybe they are reading in a second language. They prefer uncomplicated stories and vocabulary. They enjoy reading a popular series because of the text's familiarity. Many reluctant readers prefer paperbacks, magazines, and graphic novels (e.g., narrative works in comic form). If reluctant readers join book clubs, they will want these reading materials to be available (Krashen 61–62; Littlejohn "Why" 2–3; McKool; Miller and Ogranovitch).

Low-income readers. For many years, researchers stressed that family income influenced students' reading habits. Supposedly, low-income students were prone to watch more television and did not live in an environment that encouraged reading. Later, further studies proved that students from all incomes are distracted by outside school activities, television, and computers (Krashen 139–142; McKool; Zemelman et al.).

Nevertheless, what low-income students do lack are reading materials in their homes, schools, libraries, and community centers. A sponsor can provide these additional materials through donations, book sales, book fairs, paperback exchanges, and student exchanges. For the book club to succeed, the sponsor should provide high-interest reading materials, even if they are only to be shared among the members.

Increase in readers. Since 1982, the National Endowment for the Arts (NEA) has conducted studies on American adult readers. For the first time, in January 2009, American adults were reading more, and the biggest increase was in the age group 18–24-year-olds (Giola). This is significant progress, perhaps demonstrating that teachers, librarians, and book club sponsors encouraged many of these readers in their younger years. These young adults continued reading in spite of the media revolution. Educators need to build on the increase in reading by providing multiple reading activities and media.

Summary. Student book clubs are perceived as teacher-directed literature circles; the teacher usually chooses the book and prepares the discussion questions. These literature circles were developed in conjunction with the Whole Language program of using literature to teach reading. These book groups have limited numbers of participants, all of whom share the same reading level or age. Most of these literature circles have excellent results (Daniels 1–6, 30–39).

However, a group-read or literature circle has its limitations. There are several reasons for this, including these:

◆ **Reading choice.** First of all, educators should be wary of forcing children and young adults to read assigned books. According to the research, this does not encourage lifelong reading. Instead, providing high-interest books and materials to all, especially in impoverished areas, may be the answer.

◆ **Entertaining reading activities.** Reading activities are just as important as other school activities, but these activities have to be entertaining and varied.

◆ **Extrinsic rewards.** Educators should consider any extrinsic rewards questionable, unless all participants receive the same useful artifact, such as a bookmark or certificate. Even contests should be carefully considered so that every participant receives encouragement. Although reading acceleration programs are used throughout American schools, librarians need to carefully consider whether providing extrinsic rewards produces long-term results.

◆ **Test scores.** Can critical thinking be accurately tested? Progress in many skills is not testable, such as developing the imagination, patiently and persistently solving long-term problems, and learning cooperative skills. Test scores represent one day in a student's educational life. Instead of focusing on test results, educators need to consider the benefits of developing lifelong learners and readers.

◆ **Custom-designed readers.** Most important, encouraging leisure reading need not involve investing in time-consuming and expensive programs. All readers require encouragement, individually, one by one. By providing high-interest reading materials to the students and discussing their various selections, educators allow reading to be student-driven rather than teacher-driven.

Works Cited

Daniels, Harvey. *Literature Circles: Voice and Choice in the Book Clubs and Reading Groups.* 2nd ed. Portland, ME: Stenhouse, 2002. Print.
 Provides information on reading research, along with helpful suggestions about student choice and reading activities.

Giola, Dana. "Reading on the Rise." *National Endowment for the Arts.* Web. 3 June 2010.
 Reading is on the rise, especially for people ages 18–24.

Krashen, Stephen. *The Power of Reading: Insights from the Research.* 2nd ed. Westport, CT: Libraries Unlimited, 2004. Print.
 Must-read book that examines reading research, stressing the importance of student choice of reading materials. Visit author's Web site at www.sdkrashen.com and read "88 Generalizations about Free Voluntary Reading."

Littlejohn, Carol. "The Oprah Revolution: Book Clubs in Library Media Centers." *Library Media Connection* Nov./Dec. 2006: 28–29. Print.
 Discusses how school media specialists are running successful book clubs.

Littlejohn, Carol. "Why Booktalks Work." In *Keep Talking That Book! Booktalks to Promote Reading,* Vol. 2. Ed. Carol Simpson. Worthington, OH: Linworth, 2000. Print.
 Chapter 1 provides research on reading attitudes, reading interests, and reading motivation.

Margolis, Rick. "Oprah's Book Club, Jr. (The Oprah Winfrey Show Asks American's Library Association for Children's Book Recommendations) (brief article)." *School Library Journal.* Web. 21 Dec. 2010.
 Originally published Sept. 1, 2000 (18), this article states Oprah's Book Club, Jr., did not have an off-the-Richter-scale impact as expected.

McKool, Sharon S. "Factors That Influence the Decision to Read: An Investigation of Fifth Grade Students' Out-of-School Reading Habits." *BNet, CBS News.* Web. 6 June 2010.
 Originally published in 2007 *Reading Improvement* (111+), this study provides valuable research on fifth-graders' reading interests and attitudes.

Miller, Jennifer, and Nicole Ogranovitch. "Using Book Clubs to Increase Multicultural Students' Interests in Reading." *Glen Forest Elementary School, Fairfax County (VA) Public Schools.* Web. 2 June 2009.
 Book clubs help multicultural students increase their reading skills and interact positively with their peers.

Smoldt, Ashley. "Book Club: Motivating Young Readers." *Reading Today* 19.3 (Dec. 2001): 10. Print.
 After sponsoring a fourth-grade book club, the author believes all students can increase their reading skills and resolve textual issues by participating in a book club.

Zemelman, Steve, Harvey Daniels, and Marilyn Bizar. "Sixty Years of Reading Research—but Who's Listening?" *ERIC*. Web. 5 June 2010.

    Originally published in 1999 in *Phi Delta Kappan* (513), this article states that, although there are at least six decades of studies about reading attitudes and interests, teachers are not practicing the research. Many reasons for this are discussed, as are possible solutions: combining whole language with drills, being a "kid watcher," and using individualized instruction.

CHAPTER 2

Back to Our
(Book) Sponsors:
The Adult Leaders

This chapter looks at role of the book club sponsor. The chapter begins with a how-to list for the novice. Next, experienced sponsors offer suggestions for running a successful book club. The "Trouble-shooting" and "Fun Activities for All Ages" include helpful (mostly free) tips from experienced sponsors. Finally, age-specific activities conclude this chapter. Each age requires different activities, different books, and different rules. Experienced sponsors offer suggestions for each age group.

A Book Club Sponsor's Role

Sponsor requirements. A book club sponsor can be anybody who loves to read and enjoys the age group to be included in the club. Sponsors may be parents, grandparents, senior citizens, church leaders, and, of course, teachers and librarians. The sponsor is the leader of the group and defines the focus and outcome of the book club. She chooses the goals, agenda, setting, and reading activities with a light touch that includes everyone. A sense of humor is an essential requirement.

Goals. Goals can be as lofty as developing lifelong readers or as simple as just enjoying the fun of reading. Whatever goals you choose, these goals are the purpose of the group. You don't need to share these goals or even write them down. Just what do you, as the adult leader, want to accomplish?

Setting. The setting should always be in a safe but inviting space. There is more discussion on this later in this chapter and in chapter 3, "Make It Work! The Place Setting."

Support. Make certain that administrators are in agreement about the location and goals of the book club. They may also offer suggestions for books, speakers, field trips, and other activities.

More important, if problems do arise, the book sponsor may have an ally in the administration if they have agreed to its guidelines in advance.

Teacher input. A sponsor needs positive support from teachers and librarians to run a successful book club. Tell them about your plans, and get their input.

Type. What type of book club will you sponsor? Will it be for everyone, or will there be restrictions (gender-specific groups, coed groups, specific ages, size or numbers, parent-child)? Consider including all types of readers, including reluctant readers, second-language readers, and special education students. These students are sometimes the most in need of book clubs and are usually excluded.

Theme. Many sponsors are using themes like anime, storytelling, graphic novels, mystery, or poetry. (See chapter 5, "Reading Activities: The Fun Begins" for specific suggestions.)

Size. You may decide to limit the number of members. Some sponsors suggest 15–20 members for each club, but the sponsor can divide the students into separate groups to meet on different days. You can separate the group by grade, gender, or book genre.

Parents. The younger readers may need adult permission to join the club. A sample *Book Club Permission Slip* is provided at the end of the book.

Meetings. Some book clubs meet once a week, others once a month or bimonthly. A group-read club usually meets monthly to give participants time to read the selected book.

Volunteers. Volunteers add to a group, but give them choices, too. Utilize parents or teachers as facilitators. The volunteers can select a book from an age-appropriate list and discuss this selected book with the group (Lovely).

Public relations. Advertise by word of mouth, blogs, school announcements, Web sites, and signs and posters in schools, libraries, and community centers. On site, display a large sign-up poster with enticing book covers and booktalks.

The First Meeting

Rules. After welcoming the group, discuss any rules, such as that participants must come prepared, having reading the book; attend all meetings; have parental permission; clean up after lunch (if the club meets during lunch); and allow everyone a chance to talk. The sponsor can design the rules and, if appropriate, have each member sign an agreement. Allow older members to contribute and add to the rules.

Agenda. The agenda provides the structure; the sponsor provides the agenda. At the beginning of each meeting, allow extra time for latecomers by:

✦ Beginning with one-minute booktalks (a *booktalk* is a brief recommendation that doesn't reveal the ending)

✦ Allowing the group to read silently until everyone arrives

✦ Encouraging participants to booktalk a book they've read, ideally with the book close by. Ask them to do their booktalk in one minute so that everyone gets a chance.

✦ Announcing the agenda at the start of each meeting. What will the group accomplish today? Will the activity be booktalks, storytelling, information about a specific genre, or a vote on the next activity?

After accomplishing the tasks, move to the reading activity, a "fun" activity that gives spark to a book club. Schedule the activity at the end of the meeting so that everyone can complete the task.

Atmosphere. Don't forget the treats. Young people appreciate food, even healthy snacks. Serve these snacks during or after the meeting. Some sponsors like matching the treats to the book or theme. For example, try using an author's favorite recipe like Edward Bloor's "Tangerine Smoothie" or Kimberly Willis Holt's "Buttermilk Pie" (Gelman and Krupp 325, 167).

T-shirts. Some sponsors order or make t-shirts for book clubbers (Black). One activity for the first or second meeting might be to select a name, design a logo, and create a t-shirt.

Troubleshooting: Avoiding Problems

Like any group activity, problems may occur in book clubs. Here are some tips for avoiding obstacles.

Funding book clubs. Some book clubs require funding for buying books. Funding can come from these sources:

✦ You may be funded by Scholastic Book Fairs, PTA funds, private funds, Birthday Club money, and bake sales.

✦ If permitted, you can organize a café shop in the school library each morning.

✦ You can contact public libraries in the area to locate multiple copies for a group-read.

✦ Try the Web site www.bookcloseouts.com for inexpensive, multiple copies of books.

Group-read. If the group is not reading the selected book, consider selecting another book or have the group silently read the book during the meeting. Discussion occurs at the end of the meeting.

"The silence" nightmare. What if the group refuses to discuss the selected book? One educator has some excellent tools to stimulate discussion, assigning students specific roles, such as

✦ Questioner

✦ Scene setter

✦ Researcher

✦ Summarizer

✦ Word wizard

Each name specifically describes the action of the book clubber. If discussions occur easily, these tasks need not be assigned (Daniels 107–134).

Book clubber challenges. What if some club members "have an attitude"? This group can include bullies, arguers, interrupters, or cross-examiners. Kunzel and Hardesty provide helpful tips (149–154):

✦ Establish boundaries at the first meeting (no racist remarks, no drugs, and no teasing), and consistently enforce them.

✦ If a student consistently crosses boundaries, look the person in the eye, and keep a strong, steady voice. For example, you can say, "I don't let people interrupt me" and then continue with your thoughts. If the interrupter continues, use stronger language each time, such as "I'm not finished talking yet."

✦ When all else fails, have a private talk and suspend any troublemakers from the next meeting.

✦ If they are sincerely remorseful, allow them back with a private warning

Parental challenges. Talk with the administrator and get her approval before selecting any book for a group-read. If you do get complaints from parents, keep your administrator in the loop. Requesting adult-signed permission slips may prevent some problems. But, if a problem does occur, the American Library Association (ALA) offers helpful suggestions:

✦ Stay calm and courteous.

✦ Listen more than you talk.

✦ Avoid talking "library jargon" about intellectual freedom for all. Instead, keep comments upbeat while sympathizing with the parent.

✦ For further suggestions, check out the ALA Web site, www.ala.org.

Fun Activities for All Ages

Here are some ideas for group projects that work with various age groups.

Time capsule. Select a waterproof container, obtain desiccant gel bags, and create written descriptions of each item on acid-free paper. Put anything into the container that describes the relevant time period, such as music, books, clothes, and hobbies. Seal the time capsule and record the location and opening date (Hamilton 71–72, 101).

Year-round peace program. The theme of peace involves geography, ecology, social studies, languages, peace prizes, and organizations like Amnesty International. One innovative school librarian suggests using "peace" as a theme throughout the school year. In September, she places handprints of the students next to a display of international figures of peace. In October, students learn 10 international words for "peace." In November, she uses *The Peace Book,* by Todd Parr. The month of peace occurs in December. During January, February, and March, the students celebrate with an art festival, poetry readings, and a collaborative book about peace. Eventually, at the end of the school year, the program concludes with the International Peace Day Picnic (Gerlach 30–32).

Audiobooks. These are useful for book clubs, especially for reluctant readers. For a group-read, you can allow the students to listen to the audiobook while reading along silently.

Book blogs. Contributing ideas to various book club blogs has become popular. In this way, the readers can be linked internationally to one book or group of readers. For an online keyword search, use "Book Club Blogspots."

Online book clubs. Using Facebook is another way to discuss books. Launched in 2008, Book Clubs have more than 6,000 members. Users can post comments about a book, write a review, and build a library of books. Other similar Web sites are Goodreads, Shelfari, JacketFlap, and Library Thing. The Barnes and Noble bookstore has online book clubs that anyone can join. To seek other current online book clubs, search under "online book clubs."

Book club resource. For useful ideas from school librarians, try the LM_NET Liserv at Syracuse University. Use the keyword search term "book clubs" at this Web site: www.eduref.org/lm_net.

For Younger Readers (Ages 3–8)

This age group is spirited, curious, and lively. One hour is usually the length of the meeting, but books and activities should be brief, with time provided for children to stretch and move. It's helpful to have several adult volunteers.

Your attention, please! Offer something small and unbreakable to pass to the young person who is talking. It could be a small beanbag, a teddy bear, or any soft object. That person is allowed to talk while holding the object. When he finishes, he passes the object to the next person who wants to participate.

"Reading passport." At the first meeting, let each young member make a reading passport on which she can stamp or glue pictures at future meetings. Keep the passports until the final meeting, and then present each member with his or her passport ("Reading Passport").

Preschool read-aloud. No age is too young for a book club. This age group is receptive to images and brief text. Reading aloud to preschoolers teaches them sequence, language, and context. One parent ran a read-aloud summer book club for girls entering the first grade. Parents read chapter books before the meeting, and, during the meeting, for fun, activities were linked to the selected book. For *Little House in the Big Woods*, by Laura Ingalls Wilder, the group made a covered wagon fort, maple cakes from an 1800s recipe, and log cabins from Popsicle sticks. For *Beezus and Ramona*, the girls drew pictures and sent them to the author, Beverly Cleary, who responded on *Ramona* letterhead. For the series *Nancy Drew and the Clue Crew*, the girls played the board game *Clue, Jr.*, after solving a fictional mystery (Gazzana).

First and second grades. This age group loves coming to the library but usually doesn't have a club of its own. Some public librarians pick up the slack by sponsoring afterschool book clubs. One librarian formed a book club that met during the school year for about an hour a week. After hearing a story, the children were given an opportunity to discuss their reading by answering open-ended questions such as "What is your favorite part of the story?" A snack was given 30 minutes into the program; the snack was usually relevant to the story. While the children were eating, the librarian told another story. She ended the hour by having the children make a craft relevant to the story (Preis 37).

Primary grades (Grades 1–3). Folktales, picture books, puppets, short movies, and poetry are recommended for this age. Children enjoy seeing a story as well as hearing it. Many folktales can be dramatized and reenacted for this age group because they enjoy dramatic moral tales.

A community blend. Sometimes combining your forces with other city organizations can be beneficial. The Chicago Public Library united with the Chicago Police Department. Together, they ran a Mystery Beat Book Club, a five-week, afterschool program for students ages 6–12. The police brought in dogs to demonstrate their canine skills, a detective to discuss crime reporting, and an officer to teach the students how to crack codes (Burnett 48). Perhaps in your community there is an organization that will provide free and fun educational programs.

Preteens

Preteens are on the fault line between avid readers and reluctant readers. When the amount of voluntary reading decreases, some young people drop reading completely from their lives. However, if reading remains "fun" or enjoyable, readers will increase their reading skills.

Reader's profile. Preteens and teens develop individual reading tastes, skills, and interests. For this age, consider distributing a *Reader's Profile* (a sample is provided at the end of the book) at the first meeting. After evaluating the individual profiles, you can decide if a group-read would be successful. If not, students can choose other reading activities.

Activities. Reading activities remain the most important tool to engage the reluctant and unskilled readers. Preteens particularly enjoy these general activities:

✦ Crafts, magic tricks, mystery games, puppet shows, Reader's Theater, and even science experiments.

✦ Book clubs that specializes in gender or genre. One middle school librarian addressed the genre craze by creating four different weekly book clubs: Monday, horror; Tuesday, fantasy; Wednesday, mystery; Thursday, Girls' Time Out (Stevenson 34–35).

✦ The latest "fads," including books, dances, clothes, and celebrities. Preteens may want to name the club after one of these fads.

✦ Dressing up in period costumes. Consider purchasing *The Book Club Kit for the American Girls Series*, a kit that provides invitations, bookmarks, and calendars (Criswell). Suggest that the girls dress in costume and role-play the characters.

Teens

By the teen years, book clubbers are usually avid readers. Unfortunately, many teens have fallen by the wayside and need a wake-up call. This age values choice. Teens are capable of selecting the books and activities. Let them take the lead. Give everyone a chance to participate and to share ideas.

Reading choices. What about a book club run by teens? In an Arizona public library, teen council members distributed a flyer that read: "Are you sick and tired of people telling what to read? Well, we're not your Mom! Read what you want!" This slogan began the teen book club that meets twice a month for 90 minutes. All members read and discuss whatever they've read, but participation is not required. This group is run by teens for teens (Meyers 32).

Book reviewers. Teen readers love to have first crack at new books. Why not sponsor a Book Reviewer Club? All members must attend the first meeting so that the rules of book reviewing are explained. Each member must write three well-written reviews, with weekly opportunities to meet and discuss books. At the end of the year, a pizza party is given and the book reviews are gathered in a binder for Reader's Advisory (Joshi).

Art appreciation. Treat the teens to a wide variety of experiences: opera, art exhibits, and poetry readings. One school librarian stated, "We show foreign films once a month for our library club, and it brings in lots of students. Then we do special things for holidays—brunches, tea, Thanksgiving pies, Christmas card making, sponsoring a poetry reading for National Poetry Month, and go to the opera once a year" (Joshi).

Conclusion

✦ Sponsors run different and varied book clubs.

✦ Each sponsor can tweak the activities and books to fit the club's members.

✦ Problems can be avoided by advanced planning, such as requiring signed permission slips from parents for books and events.

✦ Preteens and teens are capable of selecting books and activities for the book club and can increase both their reading and cooperative learning skills.

Keyword search. Select the appropriate keyword search:

✦ General search: "book clubs," "online book clubs," and "book club blogspots."

✦ Specific search: "book clubs for kids," "book clubs for children," "book clubs for elementary students," "book clubs for teenagers," and "book clubs in the classroom."

Works Cited

American Library Association. "Strategies and Tips for Dealing with Challenges to Library Materials (Coping with Challenges)." *ALA*. Web. 23 Dec. 2009.
    Helpful guide for dealing with book challenges.

Black, Lydia. "HIT: T-shirt Library Reading Club Slogan." *LM_NET*. Web. 24 Aug. 2009.
    Advertise your book club by creating t-shirts.

Burnett, Sheila. "Book 'Em! Cops and Libraries Working Together." *American Libraries* 29.2 (Feb. 1998): 48+. Print.
    The Chicago Public Library works with the police department to inspire students to read.

Cleary, Beverly. *Beezus and Ramona*. New York: HarperCollins, 1990. Print.
    Recommended as group-read or read-aloud for younger readers.

Criswell, Patti Kelley, and Ali Douglas, ill. *The Book Club Kit*. American Girl Library. New York: American Girl, 2007. Print.
    Designed for ages 9–12. Provides everything you need (except costumes), including a Web site for questions.

Daniels, Harvey. *Literature Circles: Voice and Choice in Book Clubs and Reading Groups*. 2nd ed. Portland, ME: Stenhouse, 2002. Print.
    The author provides suggestions on how to conduct a book discussion.

Gazzana, Stefanie. Message to the author. 31 Aug. 2009. E-mail.

Gelman, Judy, and Vicki Levy Krupp. *The Kids' Book Club Book: Reading Ideas, Recipes, Activities, and Smart Tips for Organizing Terrific Book Clubs*. New York: Penguin, 2007. Print.
    Helpful book for those sponsoring an activity-oriented book club.

Gerlach, Jeanette E. "Peace Begins with Me—Celebrating United Nations World Peace Day." *School Library Media Activities Monthly* 25.8 (Apr. 2009): 30–32. Print.
>   Inspiring ideas for all ages, using the theme of "peace" throughout the school year.

Hamilton, Emma Walton. *Raising Bookworms: Getting Kids Reading for Pleasure and Empowerment*. Sag Harbor, NY: Beech Tree, 2009. Print.
>   Provides many helpful ideas and reading activities for all ages, including babies.

Joshi, Ish. "HIT: Library Club Ideas." *LM_NET*. Web. 24 Aug. 2009.
>   Ideas for young-adult book club.

Keene, Carolyn, and Macky Pamintuan. *Sleepover Sleuths. Nancy Drew and the Clue Crew 1*. New York: Aladdin, 2006. Print.
>   Younger readers will enjoy this series. Play *Clue, Jr.*, afterwards.

Kunzel, Bonnie, and Constance Hardesty. *The Teen-Centered Book Club: Readers into Leaders*. Westport, CT: Libraries Unlimited, 2008. Print.
>   Provides helpful ideas about working with teen-directed book clubs.

Lovely, Mary. Message to the author. 21 Aug. 2009. E-mail.

Meyers, Elaine. "Give 'Em What They Want: Putting Teens in Charge of Their Own Library Program Is a Formula for Success. (What Works)." *School Library Journal* 52.61 (June 2006): 31. Print.
>   Public librarian puts teens in charge of their book club.

Parr, Todd. *The Peace Book*. New York: Little Brown, 2005. Print.
>   Useful book for planning programs on peace.

Preis, Ann. "Going Clubbing: Book Clubs Spur Reading among First and Second Graders." *School Library Journal*. Web. 21 Dec. 2010.
>   A children's librarian uses book clubs with developing readers (in Apr. 2006: 37).

"Reading Passport." *Mr. Mailman*. Web. 21 Aug. 2009.
>   Create reading passports for each member of the club.

Stevenson, Sara. "When Bad Libraries Go Good." *School Library Journal*. Web. 22 Dec. 2010.
>   First published in *SLJ* (1 May 2005: 34–35), middle school librarians hosted book clubs during lunch and provided high-interest reading materials based on students' requests.

CHAPTER 3

**Make It Work!
The Place Setting**

Most sponsors have little input into the selected space for the book clubs. We must make do with the space we have. However, we can add certain highlights to the space to make it more inviting.

Kunzel and Hardesty offer helpful hints on setting up your place setting (32–33):

✦ **Quiet, please.** Try to place the book club in a quiet section of the space, away from the general public.

✦ **Where's the book club?** If the club meets in an unusual location, place signs or tape arrows pointing to the space or room.

✦ **Privacy, please.** Preferably, your space will be a private room with a door so that you can control the noise.

✦ **Bathroom accessibility.** Access to a bathroom is helpful.

✦ **Perfect space.** Try to design the space so that it isn't too small or too large. Add seating spaces for more people than you expect to attend. For example, if you are planning for 15 people, add seating for 18. Plan for late arrivals so that empty seats are near the entrance of the area.

✦ **Comfortable seating.** Arrange the chairs in a circle so that the group members can face one another. This is an unintimidating arrangement and provides a relaxed atmosphere. Beanbag chairs are great for younger children. Large, soft pillows are also inviting.

✦ **Appropriate table space.** If hardback chairs are the only furniture available, place a long table between all the chairs and have the students face one another. This table will give them space to place their books and will provide a large space for any reading activities.

- **Personal touches.** Add some colorful objects to the designated area to make the meeting special: fresh flowers, posters, and delicious treats. Later, you can display projects and photographs of the group.

- **Décor.** If you like, decorate the room differently for each meeting. For example, you can add a different tablecloth or poster for each meeting.

- **Permanent art.** Allow students to become involved by painting murals or designing the place setting. Of course, the administration must approve any permanent changes.

- **Available electrical outlets.** If possible, design the space so that the group can view a television screen or computer. Check for necessary audiovisual outlets.

- **Scrapbooks.** Consider bringing a camera to record each meeting. Show the photographs at the next meeting. Create a scrapbook for each year.

- **Recordings of your group.** Make a video about your book club in your place setting.

- **Displays of books, tapes, and magazines.** Load a book cart of appropriate books, magazines, and books on tape. Give quick booktalks on these high-interest materials.

- **Changes of location.** Not all book clubs need to meet indoors. On nice days, move the book club outside.

- **Meet and eat.** Book clubbers enjoying bringing their lunch to a quiet place during lunchtime. For many, the cafeteria is noisy and disruptive. Being able to escape from this atmosphere is a pleasure to most students.

- **The Breakfast Club.** Why not meet during mornings before school? Call your group "The Breakfast Club," and serve healthy snacks.

Keyword search. For further online information, search "library space."

Works Cited

Kunzel, Bonnie, and Constance Hardesty. *The Teen-Centered Book Club: Readers into Leaders*. Westport, CT: Libraries Unlimited, 2006. Print.

   Highly recommended book for the teen sponsor, offering many creative ideas, not only on library space but also on sponsoring a successful teen book club.

CHAPTER 4

The Book Clubbers:
Let's Go Clubbing!

Book clubbers are the members of the book club, regardless of age. Surprisingly, some educators ignore their viewpoints. Instead, educators examine test scores, standards, methods, and procedures but overlook the book club's vital element—yes, the book clubbers. Any successful book club needs their input.

This chapter begins with ideas on how to attract book clubbers to your club. Later, some book clubbers share their insights about book clubs. Finally, we describe how, by using a *Reader's Profile* for preteens and teens, you can determine the group's pulse and focus. (A reproducible *Reader's Profile* is provided in the back of the book.)

Attracting Book Clubbers

Avid readers will always be attracted to a book club. Just provide a day, spot, and time. They'll be there. However, it may take more thought to attract reluctant readers. What about second-language students or students who have special needs? These students go to libraries only for class research, hardly a pleasant experience. Educators need to be crafty and canny to seduce reluctant readers into reading.

Booktalk in classrooms. If possible, go to classrooms and urge students to join by telling them of the activities planned or, if you're comfortable with this, that students will determine the activities. Bring along some high-interest books to booktalk.

Speak at school assemblies. Speak at assemblies to attract potential members who wouldn't consider joining a book club.

Use public announcements. If the club is to be located in a school, read a one-minute book-talk during public announcements. Better yet, get a student to read or write a booktalk, welcoming students to the book club.

Talk to students. If you are in a school, talk with individual students about their favorite books and urge them (and their friends) to join the book club.

Offer treats. Mention that you plan to offer special treats or prizes for attending the first meeting. That might bring in some reluctant (but hungry) readers.

Bring a friend. Offer special treats or rewards for bringing a friend.

Write it up. Write about the book club on the school Web site under "Announcements" or "Current News." Don't put your announcement only on the library home page because the intended audience may not visit the site.

Book Clubbers Have Their Say

The book clubbers are the book club. Without their input, the book club is just an unfilled wish of the sponsor. Here are some opinions offered by several book clubbers about what they liked about their book club:

✦ "I liked talking about books and hearing other readers' opinions on books that I liked as well as books that they liked. I also liked being introduced to new books."

✦ "Personally, I loved the book club. Before I joined the club in seventh grade, I would read only a couple of chapters of a book. During the meetings, the discussions were structured so perfectly that you did not feel as if you were in a middle school, but at a higher level of learning, which is why I think I grew as a reader in the club. Now I feel I read more than just mandatory reading for class."

✦ "I was around people that I liked. They critiqued the book that I wrote and I didn't have to worry what they would say."

✦ "The mystery game had to be my favorite activity, even though I remember being camera shy when we taped it. Movies were good as well because what the authors write and how filmmaker do the movies are usually different."

✦ "I really like the format of allowing each person in the group to read their own choice of books. I'm not surprised that the group-read would be difficult for middle-schoolers, especially in our society that continues to reflect the value of individualism in every corner. Even so, it seems invaluable just to *share*, in general."

✦ "I wish they had a book club in my school."

✦ "I'm in a Mother Daughter Book Club. It's really fun!"

Book clubbers also have ideas on how to improve book clubs:

✦ "I would make it stricter against students who take advantage of it for purposes to get out of classes in order to go on field trips, miss class, or skip lunch. If I were to add anything I would try to have a longer period to work and to discuss. Maybe even adding a book the whole group can read and discuss as a great enrichment activity. The group worked so well that I would love to know how we would have done with a larger discussion with other school districts and discuss how we work and what we do versus what they do. We could have built from each other's ideas and maybe even meet for something related to literature."

✦ "The only thing I didn't like about it was the school didn't seem to appreciate us. We could have done million more things, but schools are bad with creativity and letting people have their own minds."

✦ "The time was too short. I wanted to go on field trips and I thought the book club should, at some point, touch on cross culture books. Upon coming to college, I have read many books with people in different cultures, socioeconomic situations, and times. While I know that it is usually left to the English or Social Studies department to educate students on such topics, I feel that recreational or extracurricular activities should work on this as well. Middle schools and high schools are meant to prepare students for the global community that is college and eventually the 'real world.' And, even if a book club isn't associated with a school (sponsored by a local library or bookstore), the organizer of the book club should introduce books that deal with such topics. Education is a lifelong process that adults should further. One way to do that is by reading a variety of books rather than just focusing on 'their thing.'"

✦ "Also, we could have formed certain small groups for five or ten minutes and talk about a specific genre we loved. Like, one person read *Demon in my View* by Amelia Atwater Rhodes. I loved that book, but some others didn't because it wasn't a book they liked. I am and always will be a horror fanatic. I would have liked to talk in more detail with other horror lovers. Also, the amount of time of the book club was too short."

✦ "I didn't like that there were 50 of us. It was too much."

✦ "I was in 1 [*sic*]. With a bunch of my friends. But a girl in our grade just invited herself in without her [*sic*] permission. That made all of us mad."

Summary of Responses

The book clubbers offered excellent pointers that might guide you in sponsoring your book club:

✦ Arrange extra field trips along with multiple reading activities.

✦ Add multicultural books.

✦ Set aside at least an hour for a book club meeting.

✦ Interact and exchange ideas with other schools.

✦ During some meetings, separate the book club members into smaller groups to facilitate discussion of a favorite book or genre.

✦ Be strict with disruptive book clubbers.

✦ Seek support of school administrators for your book club.

The Reader's Profile

Younger Readers (ages 3–8). Younger readers need more direction from the sponsors than do older book clubbers. They are more open to different stories and genres. Therefore, the *Reader's Profile* presented in the back of the book may not be effective for them. Instead, conduct a short discussion about their favorite books and activities. If possible, list their choices on paper or board to stimulate discussions.

Preteens and Teens. The *Reader's Profile* is designed for older readers and can be distributed at the first meeting. At this age, students read at different levels with multiple reading interests and are selective in their reading choices. The results of the survey should determine the club's future activities. The comments can be shared anonymously with the group at the next meeting.

When first distributing the survey, explain each question and describe each activity. Answer any questions no matter how long it takes. Following are some quick suggestions to save you time.

Favorite book. Book clubbers are asked to list their favorite book. Explain that it doesn't matter what kind of book they select, even a comic book. By answering honestly, the group can plan a direction for the club. The sponsor also gains knowledge of the reading level and interests of the group. Even answers about book clubbers' favorite book, series, author, and genre will yield revealing insights.

Favorite formats. Book clubbers are asked to list their preferred reading or listening format: hardback, paperback, graphic novels, books on tape or CD, online books, or magazines. Stress that they can select as many options as they like. Librarians can also use this information when ordering materials for the library.

Favorite activities. Each member circles each activity of interest, regardless of the number of activities. Explain each activity in depth, and answer any questions. (These reading activities are listed alphabetically in chapter 5.)

Anonymous results. Some members may not wish to reveal their reading interests. Don't require that they list their names; only their age and grade is necessary. At the second meeting, try to generalize the survey findings. The sponsor could say, "Four of you like to read graphic novels; seven of you like books on tape or CD."

A reproducible *Reader's Profile* can be found in the back of the book.

Works Cited

Atwater-Rhodes, Amelia. *Demon in My View*. Den of Shadows 1. New York: Laurel, 2001. Print.

Bastone, Sarah. "Comments?" Message to the author. 7 July 2009. E-mail.

Helides, Marissa. "Hello!" Message to the author. 16 July 2009. E-mail.

L., Jennifer. "Book Clubs." *Shelfari*. Web. 22 Aug. 2009.

Mann, Michael. "Comments?" Message to the author. 12 July 2009. E-mail.

My Circle Will Rule You (Lil T). "Book Clubs." *Shelfari*. Web. 23 Aug. 2009.

Quaglia, Jordan. "Hi." Message to the author. 25 Aug. 2009. E-mail.

CHAPTER 5

**Reading Activities:
The Fun Begins**

These reading activities are listed alphabetically for easy access. Each activity gives a projected age range. You may require a specific grade range:

Grades K–3 = Ages 5–8

Grades 4–6 = Ages 9–12

Middle school = Ages 13–15

High school = Ages 16+

Feel free to use any of the activities suggested, even if they are not listed in the age range for your club. You know your group's strengths, reading experiences, and attitudes. For current updates on these reading activities, check out this Web site: www.carollittlejohn.com.

ARTS AND CRAFTS

For All Ages

Arts and crafts always provide a lift to any book club and can be used for all ages. Introduce a craft at the end of each meeting, or conduct a contest for the best arts and crafts. Use resourceful Web sites that offer free, inspiring crafts for all ages ("Crafts for Kids"; "Project Ideas"; "Free Crafts").

Teaching Strategies

In order to make this activity successful and enjoyable, try these tips:

Collecting supplies. As early as possible, collect supplies that will be useful, such as paper bags, string, ribbon, glue, Popsicle sticks, material, scissors, pens, rulers, and plastic bottles. Ask the group to participate in collecting the necessary supplies.

Cleaning up. Some of these projects can be messy. Ask the group to clean up at the end of the meeting. Have a bucket of soapy water or disposable hand wipes available, along with dry towels.

Example not necessary. Do not show the completed project beforehand. Just provide the instructions and materials, and then let the club members use their imagination. They might create something better than the original design.

Age-appropriate. Select an age-appropriate project.

Benefits. Arts and crafts projects have both short-term and long-term benefits. Remember, members may gain critical-thinking skills that may not be immediately seen: in creativity, in problem solving, and in learning spatial relationships.

Dewey number. Try 736.982 for a start, but projects are scattered throughout the library.

Keyword search. To find current Web sites that offer ideas for projects, search "arts and crafts for kids," "arts and crafts for toddlers," and "arts and crafts for teens."

Works Cited on "Arts and Crafts"

"Crafts for Kids." *Enchanted Learning*. Web. 4 Oct. 2009.
> If you join Enchanted Learning for a nominal fee, you can access its entire Web site with print-friendly pages and no advertisements.

"Crafts for Kids: Arts and Crafts Ideas: Free Printable Coloring Pages for Children's Activities for Kids: Kid's Crafts Projects Directory." *AHC Arts and Crafts: Helping Kids with Arts*. Web. 4 Oct. 2009.
> Hundreds of free ideas, including coloring pages, free art resources, and craft projects.

"Free Crafts for Kids—Fun Family Craft Projects and Activity Ideas." *About.com*. Web. 4 Oct. 2009.
> Many free innovative crafts sorted by holiday, material used, topic, or type.

"Project Ideas." *The Knack*. Web. 4 Oct. 2009.
> Go to the "Projects" list.

AUTHORS, AUTHORS!

For All Ages

One way to invigorate a book club is to invite an author to speak to your group or school. If this is not feasible, consider conducting a virtual author visit. This online visit eliminates traveling expenses. However, if this is still outside your budget or technical skills, try corresponding by mail with a favorite author. All these ideas are discussed with some guidelines and Web sites to help you select appropriate programs. A quick timeline follows that will guide you through an author's visit; for a detailed list, a reproducible *Guest Speaker Checklist* is provided at the back of the book.

Author's Visit

An author's visit takes much preparation, but it is worth the effort. Here are some suggestions for having a successful visit:

Selecting the author. The author must be a perfect match for the group, by age, reading abilities, and interests. Whom does the group recommend? If the group members seem enthusiastic, they will probably enjoy the author (Gutman).

Cost. Set the budget, including the honorarium, transportation, hotel, and meal costs. If the fee is more than you afford, check with the administration for rules about fund-raisers, involving the group with your progress. To eliminate hotel and meal expenses, an adult can volunteer to host the author at his house. Booking a local author will also save transportation and hotel costs.

Contacting the author or publisher. Many author and publisher Web sites provide booking information. Book the author at least six months in advance. Include all contact information, such as date, location, audience, contact name, and phone number. Be certain to confirm details in writing, including the fee, accommodations, and an event calendar. Remain in contact with the author until the scheduled event.

Involving the community. A quick checklist of important contacts (Gutman):

- ✦ Write articles about the event, and speak to interested groups.
- ✦ Ask teachers to include books by the author in their classroom assignments.
- ✦ Have students prepare posters and signs welcoming the author.
- ✦ Consider sponsoring a poster contest presenting the author's books.
- ✦ Contact your local libraries and bookstores, and ask for their participation.
- ✦ Ask the publisher to provide free, appropriate posters, displays, or bookmarks.

The day of the event. Everything should be set up and ready to go.

- ✦ Arrive early to inspect the environment and equipment.
- ✦ Introduce the author with a brief, prepared, and enthusiastic speech.
- ✦ If required, pay the author immediately following the event.

After the event. The event is not completed until these details are finalized:

✦ Write any appreciate notes to the author, publisher, or volunteers. Include the group in this activity.

✦ Evaluate the program to correct any mistakes, using suggestions by participants.

✦ Complete any financial records.

Reproducible *Guest Speaker Checklist*. See the back of the book for the complete timeline.

Virtual Author Visit

Try connecting with an author through the Internet. It is certainly less expensive than an author's visit. Some authors will do virtual visits for no fee (Messner "Met Good Authors?").

Equipment required. A laptop computer, projector, and appropriate software are required. You can use the Skype software, which is available on Macintosh computers and PCs. A Smartboard enhances the presentation (Kerby and Chauncey). If technical difficulties occur, arrange for an "expert" (a book clubber?) to correct the problems.

Model program. One middle school teacher virtually invited young adult author Laurie Halse Anderson to her classroom to discuss *Chains: Seeds of America*. About 30 students asked questions during a 45-minute visit. Students were instructed in advance to write their question on an index card and to stand in line to ask their questions. The teacher used a MacBook laptop, connected it to the projector in the auditorium, hooked the computer into the school network, and patched it into the sound system. She used the Skype software system to connect with the author. Regrettably, some students' voices were not heard when they were asking questions, and the computer occasionally "crashed." To correct this, the teacher advises testing Skype before the presentation (Messner "Kate's Book Blog").

Letter to the Author

If technology is unavailable, don't despair. Corresponding with an author by "snail" or e-mail may be more rewarding. A letter from an author is tactile and, therefore, more personal to readers.

Sometimes an author's letter can produce devoted fans. Young adult mystery writer Lois Duncan suffered a personal tragedy when her daughter was murdered, in 1989. Her 1992 book *Who Killed My Daughter?* compared her earlier mysteries (*I Know What You Did Last Summer*; *The Third Eye*) to the horrendous details of her daughter's real-life murder. After reading the book, one librarian sent a letter to Duncan, expressing sympathy. Duncan responded in a heartfelt letter, inspiring the librarian to booktalk all of Duncan's books to young adults. The mixture of mystery and drama intrigued the students, and many became devoted fans of Lois Duncan (Littlejohn 71–74).

Keyword Search

✦ For current information on author visits, search "author visits" and "children's author visits." Also, search under the author's name, because many authors can be contacted online.

✦ To obtain current information on virtual authors, search "virtual author visits."

✦ To send a letter to an author, search the publisher online for a mailing address, then address the letter to the author "in care of" the publisher. Reputable publishing firms will forward the letter to the author.

Works Cited on "Authors, Authors!"

Anderson, Laurie Halse. *Chains: Seeds of America*. New York: Simon & Schuster, 2009. Print.
     Author is available for virtual visits. A booktalk for this book is available in chapter 6, "Cover to Cover: Recommended Group-Reads."

Duncan, Lois. *I Know What You Did Last Summer*. New York: Delacorte, 1999. Print.
     This mystery never dates. Check out the 1997 movie, too.

Duncan, Lois. *The Third Eye*. Reprint ed. New York: Delacorte, 1991. Print.
     High school senior Karen discovers she has psychic powers.

Duncan, Lois. *Who Killed My Daughter?* New York: Delacorte, 1992. Print.
     Young-adult mystery writer tries to solve the true story of her daughter's murder. This unsolved murder was featured in a 1993 TV episode of "Unsolved Mysteries."

Gutman, Dan. "The Perfect Author's Visit." Home page. Web. 7 Sept. 2009.
     Author describes the perfect author visit.

Kerby, Mona, and Sarah Chauncey. "Skype An Author's Network: Virtual Author Visits to Your Library or Classroom." *Wetpaint*. Web. 7 Sept. 2009.
     Guides novice in arranging a virtual author visit.

Littlejohn, Carol. "The Third Eye: The Strange Saga of Lois Duncan." *The Book Talker* 2 (1995): 71–74. Print.
     Describes how young-adult mystery writer Lois Duncan tries to solve the real-life murder of her daughter.

Messner, Kate. "Kate's Book Blog: Virtual Author Visits: The Good, the Bad, the Ugly, and the Awesome." *Livejournal*. Web. 7 Sept. 2009.
     Provides information on virtual author visit with Laurie Halse Anderson.

Messner, Kate. "Met Any Good Authors Lately? Classroom Author Visits Can Happen via Skype (Here's a List of Those Who Do It for Free)." *School Library Journal* Web. 21 Dec. 2010.
     This article in *SLJ* (August 1, 2009: 30–33), provides a list of authors who will participate in a no-fee virtual author visit. Also, visit Messner's home page, www.katemessner.com.

BATTLE OF THE BOOKS

For Most Readers

In the 1940s, the Chicago Public Library devised a game intended to encourage leisure reading and to develop critical-reading skills. The librarians sponsored a Battle of the Books for a local radio show. One participant, Joanne Kelly, who served as children's librarian in Urbana, Illinois, adapted the idea. The program drew interest from other librarians throughout the United States and other countries. Technology only expanded Battle of the Books. The Alaska American Association of School Librarians uses satellite television to broadcast Battle of the Books in underdeveloped areas ("Battle of the Books").

Setup. The Battle setup consists of teams of players who have read a selected number of books. As in a College Bowl, each team is asked questions about the books. The team leader (after consultation with the team) has 30 seconds to answer and is awarded points for the correct answer. After two rounds of questions about each book, the team with the highest score wins the "Battle."

Flexibility. BOB teams can consist of one person or a group. In smaller groups, book clubbers might select their favorite books for the Battle. Many larger groups are competing online with other Battle teams ("America's Battle").

Resources. Whatever the size, from preproduction to its conclusion, preparation is required. Many authors provide numerous suggestions and reproducible forms to use in order to conduct a successful Battle of the Books (Collins; Cook et al.; Kelly).

Preproduction

Participants should be at least nine years of age or have the reading skills to critically study a book. Some tips for BOB sponsors:

✦ Select 6 to 10 books that will represent all reading levels and genres. If possible, involve book clubbers in the selection.

✦ Make sure multiple copies of the books are available for teams; select paperbacks to lower costs.

✦ Divide participants into reading teams, which are expected to read all the selected books.

✦ Have the teams select a name, such as "Rapping Readers" or "Bookbugs."

✦ Require that participants attend the Battle of the Books announcement meeting for a discussion of the Battle rules.

BOB sponsors. Sponsors read all the selected books and compose several questions about each book that will be asked during the Battle. The questions are divided into easy and difficult, with several difficult "tiebreaker" questions.

For example, for the book *Going Bovine*, by Libba Bray, an easy question might be "What is the name of the character who is a video-gaming dwarf?" The correct answer is "Gonzo." A difficult question might be: "What is the title of the book that Cameron requests when she comes to the library?" The correct answer is "*Don Quixote*" (page 216). Be certain to note the page number in case the answer needs confirmation.

Production

Procedure. The Battle begins as teams sit together, with pen and paper. After the announced question, each team has 30 seconds to respond. Each team selects a team leader to write or speak the answer to the Battle sponsor.

The first round contains the easier questions, with four points given for each correct answer and one point given for the correct spelling of the author's name. The second round consists of difficult questions, with five points given for each correct answer. To settle any disputes, the answers must be provided for each question, along with the correct page number from the book.

The winning team has the most points at the end of the Battle. Prizes are optional.

Limitations. This activity denies freedom of choice in the selection of reading materials. (See chapter 1 for more information about the "battle" of free choice in reading.) Furthermore, research indicates that awarding prizes or rewards does not help develop lifelong readers. Nevertheless, if the book clubbers are excited about the activity and are involved with selecting the books, BOB can be a rewarding activity.

Agenda (Three to Four Hours)

This schedule provides a guideline for the day of the Battle (Littlejohn):

+ **Welcome.** The sponsor explains the rules and methods of the Battle.

+ **Round One.** The sponsor poses easy questions based on each of the selected books.

+ **Scoring.** Each correct answer is awarded four points; knowledge of the author of each book is awarded one point. Each team is given 30 seconds to confer and write down the answer. The sponsor then asks each team leader for the answer.

+ **Break.**

+ **Round Two.** The sponsor asks more difficult questions based on each of the selected books. Each correct answer receives five points. The sponsor asks each team leader for the answer.

+ **Tie breakers (optional).** If two or more teams tie, tie-breaking questions are asked. Each correct answer is worth one point.

+ **Scoring.** The scorekeepers need time to review the scores to make certain the scores are correct. During the scoring, the BOB participants can vote on their favorite book.

+ **Announcement.** The scorekeepers provide the sponsor with the team's scores. The sponsor announces the scores and winner.

+ **Prizes.** Prizes are optional. A certificate for each participant is one way to reward readers.

+ **Dismissal.**

Adult Participants

✦ The Battle of the Books sponsor is the reader of the questions and the final judge of the answers.

✦ The timekeeper allows 30 seconds for each answer.

✦ If needed, an adult can sponsor each team. In that case, during the Battle, that adult is responsible for announcing the team's answers.

✦ Two scorekeepers collect the written scores and tally the scores at its conclusion.

Timeline. For a comprehensive Battle of the Books Timeline, see the back of the book.

Keyword search. For current online resources, search "Battle of the Books."

Works Cited on "Battle of the Books"

"America's Battle of the Books." *America's Battle of the Books*. Web. 5 June 2010.
> For a fee, service provides rules, timeline, questions, and setup for participating schools.

"Battle of the Books." *Alaska Association of School Librarians*. Web. 19 Aug. 2009.
> AASL provides timeline, deadlines, and suggested books.

Collins, Joan. *Motivating Readers in the Middle Grades*. Columbus, OH: Linworth, 2008. Print.
> Highly recommended book for anyone who sponsors a BOB. It includes questions, reproducible forms, and timelines.

Cook, Sybilla Avery, Frances Corcoran, and Beverley Fonnesbeck. *Battle of the Books and More: Reading Activities for Middle School Students*. Fort Atkinson, WI: Upstart, 2001. Print.
> Provides questions for selected books, as well as other activities to use with small or large groups.

Cook, Sybilla Avery, Frances Corcoran, and Beverley Fonnesbeck. *Elementary Battle of the Books*. Fort Atkinson, WI: Upstart, 2005. Print.
> Provides questions for selected book titles.

Kelly, J. *The Battle of the Books (K–8)*. Santa Barbara, CA: Teacher Ideas, 1990. Print.
> Provides suggestions for book titles, along with prepared questions and answers.

Littlejohn, Carol. "AISJ Battle of the Books." Johannesburg, South Africa: n.p., 1997. Print.
> Provides agenda details for the Battle of the Books at the American International School of Johannesburg.

BOOK EXCHANGE

For All Book Clubs That Need Books

How about book clubbers exchanging books? This activity is always popular. Ask the group to bring a good book to the next meeting with a prepared, short booktalk to "sell" the book to other members.

Getting Books

Some ways to exchange book with others are as follows:

Discarded books. If you are a librarian, offer discarded books to book clubbers. If many members want the same book, devise a fair system to determine who should get the book. These books can be either kept or exchanged.

Book club exchange. Try exchanging books with other books clubs. Network with other schools and libraries. Find out which schools and libraries run book clubs in your area, contact the sponsor, and ask if exchanging books is possible. This saves expenses for both groups.

Online book exchange. Individual readers can exchange one book for another book title on-line. (However, participants must be at least 13 years of age.) The only cost is the postage. These book swaps are available online: Bookins (www.bookins.com), PaperBackSwap (www. paperbackswap.com), and Swaptree (www.swaptree.com).

Keyword search. For current online information, search "book exchange."

BOOK TRAILERS

For Preteens and Teens

Why not have the book clubbers write and digitally record a book trailer? A book recommendation from a peer is the most successful lure to promote reading. A *book trailer,* a short video that recommends a book, is similar to a movie trailer. With the permission of the book clubber, you can use these book trailers again and again to entice other readers. More important, the book clubbers will develop skills in problem solving, critical thinking, and collaboration.

Technical requirement. Making a book trailer involves much time and planning for all involved, but the product is lasting and usually satisfactory. The first requirement is access to the audio and video equipment, video cameras, mikes, computers, and computer software.

Resources. Many schools provide free technological instruction online ("Digital Video"; OET Outreach Team; "Video Editing"). Teachers can also create a book trailer using lesson plans, worksheets, and templates ("Creating a Book Trailer").

Process. Although there are multiple Web sites and books that give specific instructions, the process remains the same. Chronological steps of the process involve the four Ps (OET 3–12):

+ **Planning**
+ **Preproduction**
+ **Production**
+ **Postproduction**

These steps are general and can be used regardless of the amount or type of equipment available. Technology changes over time. Keep updated by online searches.

Planning

The planning stage involves these steps:

Define the goals.

+ Who is the intended audience? What resources are available?
+ How will all the members be involved?
+ For teachers, how will success be measured, and what are the curriculum goals?

Provide examples. Show the group some examples of good (and perhaps bad) trailers. These book trailers can be found online by searching "book trailers" and "book talks." Discuss these book trailers. What makes a good book trailer?

Size the group. All members should participate during this planning stage. Later, if the group is very large, you can divide the group into teams and have each team polish the project during preproduction, production, and postproduction. If the group is small, the book clubbers are assigned multiple tasks during each stage.

Brainstorm. Book clubbers can now "sell" their ideas on their favorite books. List the ideas, including the trailer's purpose, subject, format, length, and audience. This discussion could last for a complete meeting.

Develop the script.

✦ Who will write the script?

✦ How many actors are needed?

✦ What are the actor's lines?

✦ What images will appear?

✦ Will there be more images than dialogue?

✦ Should there be music?

✦ What about production credits?

Approve the script. The sponsor has the final word on the script, but all ideas need to be considered and democratically agreed upon.

Preproduction

Preproduction will save time and energy because it helps you anticipate and avoid any problems that might occur during production. The OET Outreach Team offers useful suggestions (6–7):

Storyboarding. A *storyboard* is a series of illustrations that represent each scene and camera shot to be included in the book trailer. These drawings show the angle of the shot and the included dialogue within each illustration. Some graphics software is available, but old-fashioned chronological drawings will work just as well. This activity is enjoyable for young artists.

The Shoot Short List. Assign someone (or a group) to make a list of available equipment, bring in the necessary props, establish the locations, and, if needed, assign actors. Be certain that all batteries are charged and that equipment is in working order.

Production

Production occurs during the actual filming. Changes can be made at this stage to improve the book trailer. However, be certain the changes meet the goals of the project (OET 7–8):

The "Logger." The logger lists the order of the filmed scenes, entering each piece of useable and deleted film in a book with the date, order, and subject.

AV Manager. The AV person or group is responsible for keeping a record of loaned equipment and props, including available replacement batteries.

Postproduction

Postproduction is the stage during which the trailer is actually created. Assign individuals to these tasks (OET 8–11):

Master log. Assign a group or person to create a master log by organizing the film footage by date, scene, take, and time of clip. Use the logging footage created during production.

Sequence footage. After the master log is finished, a group or person is responsible for sequencing the footage. This process is likely done digitally, and the end result is placed into one electronic, editable file.

Editing. This task includes both visual and sound editing. This requires software application, such as iMovie (Mac), MovieMaker (Microsoft), Adobe Premier (Mac/Win), Final Cut Pro (Mac), or Avid Xpress Pro (Mac/Win). Some software allows editing in both the visual and the sound tracks. If needed, add music and titles.

Screening. Plan a "premiere" for the group. Ask if the group wants any improvements.

Exporting. The book trailer can be placed on a Web site, DVD, or CD-ROM. (Sometimes exporting the trailer to CD or DVD may require extra software.) Save the original on a computer's hard drive so that the trailer is always available.

Evaluating. After completing the book trailer, evaluate the process with the group. Discuss any problems, and decide if the outcome was positive for the group.

Keyword search. For current online information, search "digital book trailers" and "book trailers."

Works Cited on "Book Trailers"

"Creating a Book Trailer." *Nutmeg Books*. Web. 1 Nov. 2009.
> Provides specific instructions for teachers, including worksheets, lesson plans, and templates.

"Digital Video Production." *Monroe County Intermediate School District*. Web. 10 Nov. 2009.
> Provides links to Internet resources. The "how-to" section is for both beginning and advanced students.

The OET Outreach Team. "MovieMaking in the Classroom." *Office of Educational Technology, College of Educational Technology, College of Education, University of Illinois Urbana-Champaign*. Web. 1 Nov. 2009.
> Tutorial on how to make a short movie, step-by-step.

"Video Editing: Instructor's Guide TE1141." *Curriculum and Instructional Materials Center for the Technology Education Division, Oklahoma Dept. of Career and Technology Education*. Web. 1 Nov. 2009.
> Download this PDF for a syllabus on video editing.

CREATIVE DRAMATICS

For All Ages, Especially Younger Readers

Children process the world differently because their powers of emotion and imagination are more developed than their reasoning powers. By using creative dramatics, children can learn by thinking out loud, interpreting their ideas, and interacting with others. Creative dramatics is an activity that can be used alone or as a warm-up for storytelling, Reader's Theater, puppet shows, or any dramatics. However, creative dramatics is different from drama because it uses no written dialogue; instead, the performers use a form of imaginative play.

Rules. Certain rules apply for all age groups. Martin uses these guidelines:

◆ All participants will decide their space within the predetermined space. Each participant will be respectful of his peers' space.

◆ Every participant will listen and focus her attention on the adult leader.

◆ No one will criticize another's performance.

◆ When a person talks, all will listen.

◆ Questions and suggestions can occur only after the activity.

For Younger Readers (Ages 3–8)

From an early age, children love to "dress up" and role-play. This impulsive desire can be integrated into a learning situation, either in a classroom or in a book club. Many scholars believe that creative dramatics increase learning because children can step inside the story and become a character or idea.

Ready, set, go! Start with young children standing in a circle. Try to persuade even the shyest children that they can contribute with their imagination. Perhaps you can ask the children to become a tree moving in the wind or a flower growing from its roots.

◆ **Using poetry.** Use poems or singing rhymes that involve action, such as "I'm a Little Teapot." Read a poem aloud, and encourage the children to add the sounds or actions. Collect a wide range of action stories that relate to the topic.

◆ **Use cumulative folktales.** Try a cumulative story, such as "The House That Jack Built" or "The Gingerbread Boy." Have the children act the story as a group, and ask for volunteers to perform each of the characters (John).

◆ **Share different versions of folktales.** Share picture books on the same folktale, such as "Little Red Riding Hood." *Lon Po Po* tells the Chinese version of "Little Red Riding Hood." Read the European version first and then the Chinese version. Have children act all the parts, and then select one person to perform each character: wolf, three daughters, and mother (Martin).

Preteens

Creative dramatics at this age may be more difficult because many preteens are self-conscious. Try these suggestions:

◆ **Icebreaker.** Begin with a group participation activity. Play the game "Telephone." The adult leader whispers a phrase to one of the participants, who then whispers that phrase to the next participant and so on until the phrase is whispered to the last participant. At the end of the game, players will be surprised at the final phrase. If one of the participants can't understand or hear the phrase, she can say "Operator." This phrase can be repeated up to three times. If the phrase is not understood, the player can say "Disconnected" and stop the game. The adult leader then uses another phrase and begins again (O'Rourke).

◆ **Use award-winning books.** When passages are read aloud, students can read alone or together. Simultaneous readings are known as *choral readings* and can be productive and enjoyable. Use favorites like *The Watsons Go to Birmingham—1963* by Christopher Paul Curtis or *Bridge to Terabithia* by Katherine Paterson (Kaplan).

◆ **Use myths.** Try reading a version of Pygmalion, especially the version by Bernard Evslin, Dorothy Evslin, and Ned Hoopes, in *Heroes and Monsters of Greek Myths*. After the story, the students discuss Pygmalion's role as a sculptor and as an artist. Afterward, students can play the game "Clay," also known as "Statues" or "Sculptures." One person pretends to be a piece of clay. The other children take turns gently moving the "statue" into different positions. In another game, the group moves into different positions until the group leader calls "Freeze!" The group members hold their poses until the group leader says "Move" and then stop when the leader again says "Freeze!" (O'Rourke).

◆ **Use poetry.** This is a good age at which to integrate poetry into the mix. A group leader can encourage children to use poetry as creative dramatics. Divide the children into different groups, and give each group a different poem. Each group picks one stanza from the poem and develops a skit to perform before the entire group. This skit should convey the poem's theme ("Using Creative Dramatics").

For Teens

This group is the most self-conscious because of peer pressure and of their desire to be included. However, when they relax, they can enjoy these activities:

◆ **Icebreaker.** For group participation, have the group divide into pairs and play the game "Mirrors." One partner moves into a certain position, and the other partner must imitate that pose. This activity encourages teamwork (O'Rourke).

◆ **Use social studies.** These young adults have a broader aspect of history. They can describe a historical event either as a reporter or as a historical figure. Or they can recite a song, short story, or poem relevant to a historical event (Bontempo).

◆ **Use literature.** In literature, the group can improvise characters in a poem, story, or novel. This improvisation ensures that the characters and story remain locked in the minds of the participants.

- ✦ **Explore "hot" topics.** Creative dramatics can explore current issues as gang warfare, gun control, and racism. An excellent book to explore prejudice is *Roll of Thunder, Hear My Cry*, by Mildred D. Taylor (Bontempo).

Keyword search. For online information, search "creative dramatics," "creative dramatics for children," "creative dramatics in the classroom," and "creative dramatics lesson plans."

Works Cited on "Creative Dramatics"

Bontempo. Barbara T. "Exploring Prejudice in Young Adult Literature through Drama and Role Play." *ALAN Review.* Web. 3 Oct. 2009.
>Offers numerous ways for teens to explore prejudice with drama and role-play.

Curtis, Christopher Paul. *The Watsons Go to Birmingham.* New York: Laurel Leaf, 2000. Print.
>Try this book as a choral reading.

Evslin, Bernard, Dorothy Evslin, and Ned Hoopes. *Heroes and Monsters of Greek Myths.* New York: Scholastic, 1980. Print.
>Read the myth "Pygmalion" and play "Clay."

John, Andrew P. "How to Use Creative Dramatics in the Classroom." *Childhood Education.* Web. 2 Oct. 2009.
>Provides examples of using creative dramatics in the elementary classroom.

Kaplan, Jeffrey. "Acting Up across the Curriculum: Using Creative Dramatics to Explore Adolescent Literature." *ALAN Review.* Web. 2 Oct. 2009.
>Author offers preteen creative dramatic activities in conjunction with popular adolescent literature.

Martin, Geraldine. "The Art of Creative Dramatics through the Eyes of a Young Child." *Yale–New Haven Teachers Institute.* Web. 2 Oct. 2009.
>Provides creative dramatics to be used with plays for young children.

O'Rourke, Kelley. "The Creative Dramatics Cookbook: Recipes for Playmaking." *Yale–New Haven Teachers Institute.* Web. 2 Oct. 2009.
>Although author believes creative dramatics is more successful with younger children, she offers creative dramatics for all ages, including "Telephone" and "Pygmalion."

Taylor, Mildred D. *Roll of Thunder, Hear My Cry.* New York: Penguin, 1997. Print.
>Older groups can explore racism with this Newbery winner.

"Using Creative Dramatics with the Teaching of Poetry." *A to Z Teacher Stuff.* Web. 2 Oct. 2009.
>How to use creative dramatics with poetry for grades 3–5.

Young, Ed. *Lon Po Po.* New York: Putnam, 1996. Print.
>A Chinese version of the folktale "Little Red Riding Hood."

FIELD TRIPS

For All Ages

Field trips do require some advance planning: getting signed permission slips, recruiting adult volunteers, and organizing transportation. After the field trip, the sponsor and the group might write appropriate thank-you notes. Regardless of the amount of planning, every field trip can be a learning experience for everyone, including the adults.

Field Trip Suggestions

Some suggested field trips are:

✦ **Visit discount bookstores.** Consider visiting a discount bookstore. Have each book clubber bring a nominal amount so that she can purchase books while you do some "book shopping" for the group or library.

✦ **Attend plays.** Take book clubbers to plays in the area. Prepare the group by having multiple copies of the play; if possible, provide some background to the play before attending.

✦ **Tour the libraries.** Why not take a tour to a local library? Some book clubbers may not been to a public library. Try to arrange for new patrons to apply for a library card so that they can check out books.

✦ **Tour museums and historical sites.** What historical sites and museums are available in your area? Could these sites inspire readers and writers?

✦ **Where else to go.** For a useful Web site for field tips, try A to Z Home's Cool Homeschooling, searching "field trips." This site offers suggestions on locations and will help plan your field trip.

✦ **Another helpful Web site.** Field Trip Factory teaches you how to design a free field trip according to age group. You can type in your zip code (only in the United States and Canada) for suggestions for local field trips.

✦ **Permission Form.** For a reproducible *Permission Form for Field Trips*, see the back of the book.

✦ **Keyword search.** For other Web sites, try "field trips for kids," "field trips for kindergartners," "field trips for elementary students," "field trips for middle school students," or "field trips for high school students."

Works Cited for "Field Trips"

"Field trips." *A to Z Home's Cool Homeschooling*. Web. 27 Sept. 2009.
    Search "field trips" to plan your field trip.

"Field trips." *Field Trip Factory*. Web. 27 Sept. 2009.
    Type in your zip code to find recommended field trips in your area.

GUEST SPEAKERS

For All Ages

Guest speakers add spark to any meeting. When booking a speaker, make certain you have many books, tapes, or magazines available about this person or subject. If you have time, booktalk these books. Have a list of questions prepared by you or the group to help move the conversation.

Some guest speakers worth considering are parents, grandparents, business and community leaders, coworkers, and university instructors. Some other suggestions are:

◆ A local reporter, artist, poet, or author

◆ A photographer

◆ For mystery lovers: book a detective, coroner, police officer, or any person in law enforcement

◆ A "local" celebrity, even if he has had only "15 minutes of fame"

◆ An archeologist, anthropologist, or astronomer

◆ Professional sports person

◆ A "survivor" from some tragic event, such as a war or holocaust

◆ A recovered addict

◆ A local historian

◆ Person from another country to speak about her country's culture and religion

◆ Young person who can speak about accomplishing a monumental task like writing a book or starting a community project

◆ Any other speakers who will lift or inspire book clubbers

Guest Speaker Checklist. See the back of the book for a reproducible Guest Speaker Checklist.

MYSTERY GAMES

For All Ages

The object of the mystery game is for the participants to put on their detective caps to solve a mystery, usually (but not always) a murder. Mystery games have many names: murder mystery games, detective games, and mystery games. Whatever the nomenclature, this who-done-it activity will add zest to a book club. The mystery game resembles the board game *Clue*, but the players interactively participate as the detectives.

Select the mystery. Some mystery games require only one person on a computer; others request a group from 6 to 100. Select the mystery, and decide the structure. Will detectives work as a team or as individuals?

Mystery kits. You can order mystery games through some library supply catalogs. These kits provide one mystery, one script, a list of characters, and the necessary props. You can use the game only once since the solution to the mystery is revealed to the group.

Write your own mystery. If cost is a factor, consider writing and producing a mystery related to the school or community. Each mystery should include at least six characters that possess a criminal motive. Develop several locations (e.g., school, bedroom, and police station) to hide important clues.

Videotape suspects. What about adding a personal touch to these mystery games? Ask some students and teachers (not in the group) to be the suspects. Videotape the suspects as they deliver their written lines. (For suspects who can't remember their lines, you can write cue cards.) Volunteers might agree to supply their names (as opposed to the character's name). Of course, when using the actual names of the participants, you need to receive each participant's written agreement.

Preproduction

After selecting the mystery, the sponsor plans the mystery game day with these tasks:

✦ Select an advanced date for the mystery game.

✦ Give yourself at least a month to promote and plan.

✦ Decide if you need individual detectives or detective agencies. Perhaps each team can give the agency a name.

✦ Publicize the activity many times throughout the month: via public announcements, Web site announcements, and book club announcements.

✦ Encourage the entire group to attend on the day of the game.

Production

On the day of the mystery game, arrive early to complete these tasks:

✦ Use a large area, like a school gymnasium or stage, to plant the clues.

✦ Chalk-mark the "victim," and mark off the crime scene.

◆ Begin the game on schedule or when all the detectives arrive.

◆ To begin the mystery game, play the videotape of the suspects to the detectives.

◆ Provide detectives with notebooks where they can write down clues.

◆ After an hour of looking through the clues and taking notes, have each group convene to select the "killer". The groups then provide the name to the sponsor.

◆ Announce the "murderer" and then provides a list of detectives who solved the crime.

Because this activity takes about three hours, you can do it at the end of the year, when teachers need extra time to submit grades. Prizes are optional.

Helpful Web Sites

Try these Web sites for a mystery game just right for your group:

◆ An excellent Web site that lists many resources for all ages (including writing your own mystery) is www.42explore.com/mystery.htm.

◆ Mystery games can be downloaded (at a cost) for players ages 6–adult. You can also customize your own mystery: www.mymysteryparty.com.

◆ For teacher-developed mysteries involving science, go to this inspiring Web site: www.accessexcellence.org/AE/mspot/.

For Younger Readers (Ages 3–8)

Mysteries should be brief and contain no overt violence. Consider these suggestions:

◆ **Nursery rhymes.** Use nursery rhymes as a startup. "The Queen of Hearts" is a four-line rhyme:

The Queen of Hearts she made some tarts all on a summer's day;
The Knave of Hearts he stole the tarts and took them clean away.
The King of Hearts called for the tarts and beat the Knave full sore
The Knave of Hearts brought back the tarts and vowed he'd steal no more.

To solve this mystery with the book clubbers, provide a deck of cards and eliminate the "suspects" one by one. (The Knave of Hearts is, of course, the Jack of Hearts.)

◆ **Scavenger hunt.** If solving a mystery is too advanced, plan a scavenger hunt. Plant some objects around the room before the book clubbers arrive. Divide the members into teams. Provide a picture list of hidden objects, or use a color theme as the group searches for red, green, and blue objects.

◆ **Picture mysteries.** Try the book *You're the Detective!* (Treat). Designed especially for ages 4–8, this collection contains 24 picture mysteries. The clues are in the illustrations.

◆ **Activity.** All ages love mysteries. Perhaps younger readers can select an object from a paper bag and try to guess the object. Or, before serving snacks, blindfold the participants, and ask if they can guess the snacks (Ross).

Preteens

These book clubbers have more developed reading skills and can participate in complex mysteries. Most of them know about Nancy Drew, the Hardy Boys, and other fictional detectives. You can begin the mystery by saying, "How many of you have heard of Nancy Drew [or whoever is popular]? Today we will all participate in a mystery, just like Nancy Drew."

✦ **The 39 Clues.** This mystery series, *The 39 Clues*, is created especially for grades 3–6 with a Web site that provides clues.

✦ **Crime and puzzlement.** Preteens and reluctant readers can read the *Crime and Puzzlement* series, ponder the illustrations, and solve the mystery (Treat).

✦ **Shorter mysteries.** One online game contains puzzles or short two-minute mysteries ("The MysteryNet's Kids Mysteries"). For book lovers, try the *Encyclopedia Brown* series or *Two-Minute Mysteries*, by Sobol.

✦ **60-minute games.** If you are seeking a mystery game that uses the audience as both suspects and detectives, Dramatic Fanatic has a variety of different games that last about an hour. They are usually used at birthday parties, but preteens would also enjoy this.

✦ **Other activities.** Some quick activities include taking fingerprints, writing with lemon juice, learning secret codes, and wearing disguises (Ross).

Teens

Teens are familiar with murder mysteries through books and television. This group can handle the longer mysteries, anything from two to four hours. Some adult mystery games may also be appropriate.

✦ **One-meeting mysteries.** Try *Cleverly Crafted Five-Minute Mysteries* (Weber). The murder plots are complex and require research. Have a computer available to quickly check facts. List the clues and encourage book clubbers to solve the crime.

✦ **Teen mysteries.** University Games produces Murder Mystery Party, with several boxed games of teen mysteries. These games (such as *Panic at the Prom for Teens*) require that there be no more than eight participants.

✦ **History mysteries.** Many teens are interested in real-life mysteries or conspiracies. Who killed President John F. Kennedy? What happened to the aviator Amelia Earhart? Why did the *Titanic* sink? Teens can research their findings and provide different theories about historical figures or conspiracies. Each detective or agency can compile a plausible timeline of the likely scenario, with supporting evidence.

Keyword search. For current information online, try "mystery games," "kids mystery games," "detective games," and "online mystery games."

Works Cited on "Mystery Games"

"Dramatic Fanatic Mystery Party Kits for Kids." *Dramatic Fanatic*. Web. 12 Dec. 2009.
        For ages 8–13. For a fee, participants engage in a mystery that lasts an hour. Includes character cards, hosts cards, and clues.

"My Mystery Party." *My Mystery Party*. Web. 13 Aug. 2009.
> Downloadable and boxed mystery games for all ages at a minimal cost.

"The MysteryNet's Kids Mysteries." *Kids.MysteryNet.com*. Web. 12 July 2009.
> Interactive mystery detective games that includes a "Solving Mysteries Group Worksheet."

"The Mystery Spot: Access Excellence Mysteries." *Access Excellence*. Web. 12 Aug. 2009.
> Teacher-developed mysteries based on science.

Panic at the Prom for Teens. Murder Mystery Party. New York: University Games, 2008.
> Series of boxed games developed for teens.

"The Queen of Hearts: lyrics." *Famousquotes.me.uk*. Web. 16 May 2010.
> This rhyme also appears in Lewis Carroll's book *Alice's Adventures in Wonderland*, first published in 1865.

Ross, Anjelika. "HIT: Mystery Enrichment Book Club." *LM_NET*. Web. 24 Aug. 2009.
> Inspiring ideas to use with a mystery book club.

"Scavenger Hunts for Kids." *Scavenger Hunts for Kids*. Web. 13 Aug. 2009.
> Free, printable treasure hunts, scavenger hunts, and fun games for children.

Sobol, Donald J. *Encyclopedia Brown, Boy Detective*. Encyclopedia Brown 1. New York: Puffin, 2007. Print.
> Ten-year-old Encyclopedia is a star detective. Each book in the series provides 10 mysteries for preteens to solve.

Sobol, Donald J. *Two-Minute Mysteries*. New York: Apple, 1991. Print.
> Preteens will enjoy solving these brief mysteries.

"The 39 Clues." *Scholastic*. Web. 12 July 2009.
> Online mysteries for ages 9–12. Registration is required, but participation is free.

"The Topic: Mystery." *42explore*. Web. 12 July 2009.
> Provides online resources for all ages.

Treat, Lawrence, and Leslie Cabaroa, ill. *Crime and Puzzlement: 24 Solve-Them-Yourself Picture Mysteries*. Book 1. New York: Godine, 2003. Print.
> For preteens, these picture mysteries offer clues to help them solve the crime. Also, try *Crime and Puzzlement 2* (1982); *Crime and Puzzlement 3* (1988).

Treat, Lawrence, and Kathleen Boroik, ill. *You're the Detective! Twenty-Four Solve-Them-Yourself Picture Mysteries*. New York: Godine, 2004. Print.
> Younger readers solve mysteries by finding clues in the illustrations.

Weber, Ken. *Cleverly Crafted Five-Minute Mysteries*. New York: Running, 2007. Print.
> Teens will enjoy these quick-solving mysteries. Also, try the sequel, *Even More Five-Minute Mysteries* (2008).

ONE-MINUTE BOOKTALKS

For Preteens and Teens

Booktalks are "commercials" for books that don't reveal the ending. Each booktalk should grab the students' interest by introducing the book's scenes or characters. With one-minute booktalks, you can cover at least five books quickly and effectively. Encourage the book clubbers to compose one-minute booktalks on their favorite books.

The following pages will provide examples of booktalks. The booktalks are divided into two age groups (preteens and teens), arranged alphabetically by the author's last name. Each reproducible booktalk suggests *related books* for those who want another choice or to read similar books. The *note* at the end of each booktalk provides relevant information for sponsors and offers additional material, including (at times) the ending.

Keyword search: To discover current books and resources, try "booktalks," "book talks," and "book trailers."

BOOKTALKS

Preteens

Beil, Michael D. *The Red Blazer Girls: The Ring of Rocamadour*. New York: Knopf, 2009. Ages 9–12.

Mystery.

Related books: *The Red Blazer Girls: The Vanishing Violin* by Michael D. Beil; *The Westing Game* by Ellen Raskin; *Mudshark* by Gary Paulsen; *Danny Dunn* series by Jay Williams.

Booktalk: Want to read a great mystery? Better yet, do you want to solve a great mystery? Come along with the Red Blazer Girls to decipher the clues in a rare treasure. Sophie, Margaret, and Rebecca are called the Red Blazer Girls because they wear their red Catholic school uniforms. When they're not in school, they are solving mysteries. Join them and help solve the mystery.

Note: The three girls meet an elderly lady in the attic of a church. She asks the girls to explain an old birthday card from her estranged daughter. The plot is filled with puzzles—linguistic, mathematical, and logical. Even the bibliographic information must be read in a mirror. Not the ordinary, run-of-the-mill mystery series.

Brunvand, Jan Harold, Robert Loren Fleming, and Robert F. Boyd Jr. *The Big Book of Urban Legends*. New York: Paradox, 1994. Ages 9+.

Graphic novel; horror.

Related books: books by Jan Harold Brunvand; *Scary Stories* series by Alvin Schwartz.

Booktalk: This comic book describes 200 horror stories that are just too good to be true. That's what makes them urban legends. Learn about the vanishing hitchhiker, the choking Doberman, and the Mexican pet. These stories will just kill you!

Note: This book can be part of a Reader's Theater activity. See chapter 5 for RT script "Too Good to Be True" and add another urban legend to the script.

Dannenberg, Barry. *Shadow Life: A Portrait of Anne Frank and Her Family.* New York: Scholastic, 2005. Ages 9–12.

Biography.

Related books: *The Diary of a Young Girl* by Anne Frank; *Anne Frank: Beyond the Diary, a Photographic Remembrance* by Ruud Van der Rol et al.; *Anne Frank: The Biography* by Melissa Muller et al.

Booktalk: Anne Frank and her family lived secretly in an attic or annex in Europe during World War II. Why? Because they were Jewish and were ordered to a concentration camp to be murdered. One sad day, someone reported the families to the Nazis. All died except Anne's father. He was given Anne's diary. Now everyone knows Anne Frank. Find out her amazing story.

Note: This book is different from other books about Anne Frank because the author creates a fictional diary by Anne's older sister, Margot. Apparently Margot had a diary, too, although her diary was destroyed. Using this technique, the author is able to present a well-rounded, fuller picture of life in the secret annex in Amsterdam, also providing details about the deaths of the families.

Ellis, Deborah. *Our Stories, Our Songs: African Children Talk about AIDS.* Markham, Ontario, Canada: Fitzhenry and Whiteside, 2005. Ages 9–12.

Nonfiction.

Related books: *Children of AIDS: Africa's Orphan Crisis* by Emma Guest; *Teens with AIDS Speak Out* by Mary Kitteredge; *Ryan White: My Own Story* by Ryan White.

What is life like for children surrounded by the daily problem of AIDS? In sub-Saharan Africa, there are more than 11.5 million orphans. Some live on the streets, some are in jail, and some care for their brothers and sisters. Each person has a story. Come and meet them. They might surprise you.

Note: This book contains personal stories and photographs of young people who have been affected by the AIDS virus. Includes sidebars of pertinent information about child labor, orphans, and symptoms of AIDS. Long after the book is finished, the stories of these young people remain.

Kinney, Jeff. *Diary of a Wimpy Kid: The Last Straw.* New York: Amulet, 2009. Ages 9–12.

Graphic novel.

Related books: *Diary of a Wimpy Kid* series by Jeff Kinney; *Sweet Farts* by Raymond Bean; *Lawn Boy* by Gary Paulsen.

Booktalk: I'm Greg Heffley. I'm a good kid, the best. No one thinks so because I'm always messing up. Like the time I got chocolate on the back of my pants. How embarrassing. I had to wear Mom's sweater tied around my pants as we went to church. I just hope I look good in pink!

Note: This hilarious "novel in cartoons" is a perfect selection for a reluctant reader. The protagonist relates all of his experiences in his diary, and each experience is a hoot. Much of the humor is bathroom humor, but the young readers (especially boys) will love it.

Nelson, Kadir. *We Are the Ship: The Story of Negro League Baseball.* New York: Hyperion, 2008. Ages 9+.

Sports; nonfiction.

Related books: *Heroes of the Negro League: Only the Ball Was White* by Jack Morelli and Mark Chiarello; *Satchel Paige: Striking Out Jim Crow* by James Sturm and Rich Tommaso; *Baseball: An Illustrated History* by Geoffrey C. Ward and Ken Burns.

Booktalk: For many years African Americans could not play major league baseball. In 1920, they formed the Negro League. Some of the world's greatest baseball players played in the Negro League: Hank Aaron, Satchel Paige, Willie Mays, and Jackie Robinson. Other great baseball players played in the Negro League, but we may not know their names. Here is their courageous story. As one baseball player stated, "We are the ship; they are the sea."

Note: This oversized, beautifully illustrated book should be in all libraries, regardless of the reader's age. The author presents its narrative as a collective voice, making the text intimate and revealing. Includes bibliography and author's note.

Rallison, Janette. *My Fair Godmother.* New York: Walker, 2009. Ages 9–14.

Fantasy.

Related books: *Princess of the Midnight Ball* by Jessica Day George; *How to Ditch Your Fairy* by Justine Larbalestier; *Just One Wish* by Janette Rallison; *Dragon Bait* by Vivien Velde.

Booktalk: Notice how this book is titled *My Fair Godmother* instead of *My Fairy Godmother*? Well, Savannah's godmother is only "fair" at her job of magic. Savannah asks for a true prince to take her to the prom. Big mistake! Savannah goes back in time as Cinderella and Snow White. With only one wish left, can Savannah make it back to modern times?

Note: This humorous book is perfect for girls who are still swept away by the magic of romantic fairy tales.

Scieszka, Jon, ed. *Guys Write for Guys Read.* New York: Viking, 2005. Ages 9–12.

Short stories.

Related books: *The Stinky Cheese Man and Other Stories* by Jon Scieszka; *The Dangerous Book for Boys* by Conn Iggulden and Hal Iggulden; *The Pocket Dangerous Book for Boys* by Conn Iggulden and Hal Iggulden.

Booktalk: Okay, guys, this one's for you. This one has it all: short stories, poems, comics, and drawings. Who says guys don't read? Read this, and prove everyone wrong.

Note: According to reading studies, most reluctant readers are male in gender. For further information, check out www.guysread.com.

Sensel, Joni. *The Farwalker's Quest.* **New York: Bloomsbury, 2009. Ages 9–12.**

Science fiction.

Related books: *The Giver* and *Gathering Blue* by Lois Lowry; *Sea of Trolls* by Nancy Farmer; *The Hunger Games, Catching Fire*, and *Mockingjay* by Suzanne Collins.

Booktalk: Ariel and her best friend, Zeke, are beginning their trades as Healtouch and Tree-Singer. Suddenly they discover a magical dart with strange symbols carved on it. Behold! Their adventure begins. On their journey, whom will they find? Who knows? Maybe they'll discover their own identities.

Note: Although this novel seems to occur in the far distant past, the plot actually occurs after an apocalyptic war destroys all technology and blinds humankind. As villagers gain their sight, they struggle to learn their trades. Twelve-year-old Ariel and Zeke believe they know their destinies, but, after finding the dart, they are kidnapped and forced on their perilous journey. Ariel discovers that she is actually a Farwalker, a guide who carries messages to villages.

Stone, Tanya Lee. *Almost Astronauts: 13 Women Who Dared to Dream.* **Somerville, MA: Candlewick, 2009. Ages 9+.**

Nonfiction.

Related books: *Moonshot: The Flight of* Apollo 11 by Brian Floca; *Sally Ride* by Linda R. Wade; *Sally Ride: Space Pioneer* by Lorraine Jean Hopping.

Booktalk: Can women become astronauts? Of course they can. In 1983, Sally Ride became the first American woman in space. But, decades earlier, other American women participated in astronaut testing. In 1960, 13 women were tested and all were rejected as astronauts, even though they tested higher than the male applicants did. Why were they rejected? Because they were women. In 1962, who testified before Congress that women were incapable of becoming astronauts? A woman.

Note: This large-size, photo-essay book gives a riveting look at the struggles women pilots faced as they sought admission to the NASA space program. Jerrie Cobb has a fascinating biography because she passed all the tests and even flew more miles than John Glenn. Vice President Lyndon Johnson stopped any discussion of admitting women into the space program. Why? He was afraid other "minorities" would apply. Highly recommended.

Sturm, James, Andrew Arnold, and Alexis Frederick-Frost. *Adventures in Cartooning.* **New York: First Second, 2009. Ages 9–12.**

Graphic novel.

Related books: *Robot Dreams* by Sara Varon; *Sardine in Outer Space* series by Emmanuel Guibert and Joann Sfar; *Little Vampire* series by Joann Sfar.

Booktalk: Want to know how to draw cartoons? Here's the book that show you how to turn your doodles into comics!

Note: This graphic novel won't require much booktalking. Just show the book and watch the magic of a disappearing book. Within the plot of a dragon, knight, and princess, the authors show how to draw cartoons and make them understandable to readers.

Time *1969: Woodstock, the Moon, and Manson: The Turbulent End of the '60s,* **eds. of** *Time.* **40th Anniversary special. New York: Time, 2009. Ages 12+.**

Nonfiction.

Related books: *1969: The Year Everything Changed* by Rob Kirkpatrick; *Woodstock Revisited* by Susan Reynolds; *Boom! Talking about the Sixties* by Tom Brokaw.

Booktalk: Want to read a far-out book that has some cool photos? Learn about Woodstock, Sesame Street, and the Beatles. See the first moonwalk—not Michael's dance step but the first step on the moon. This book may blow your mind!

Note: Many scholars believe that that the 1960s changed American history and that Americans are still reeling from its lessons. This book offers short essays with descriptive photographs and is highly recommended for interested readers.

Walker, Paul Robert. *Remember Little Rock: The Time, the People, the Stories.* **Washington, DC: National Geographic, 2009. Ages 9–12.**

Nonfiction.

Related books: *The Power of One* by Judith Bloom Fraden; *Warriors Don't Cry* by Melba Pattillo Beals; *Through My Eyes* by Ruby Bridges and Margo Lundell; *If a Bus Could Talk: The Story of Rosa Parks* by Faith Ringold.

Booktalk: "Two, four, six, eight/We're not going to integrate." This was the rallying cry of a mob of whites who didn't want African Americans to attend high school with them. On September 4, 1957, in Little Rock, Arkansas, the world saw an ugly side of American life. Nine students were denied entry into the school and faced a threatening mob. Here are their stories. Never forget to *Remember Little Rock.*

Note: This thin book with memorable photographs tells the horrific stories of nine teens who were threatened only because they were African Americans who wanted to attend a better school than the segregated school they were supposed to attend. The author interviews many of the participants and concludes with an epilogue, a civil rights timeline, and postscripts from the participants.

Walker, Sally M. *Written in Bone: Buried Lives of Jamestown and Colonial Hartland*. Minneapolis, MN: Carolrhoda, 2009. Ages 10+.

Nonfiction.

Related books: *Corpses, Coffins and Crypts* by Penny Colman; *Grave Matters* by Nigel Burley; *Celebrations of Death* by Peter Metcalf and Richard Huntington, eds.; *The Bone Lady* by Mary M. Manheim.

Booktalk: Did you know that each unmarked grave is a mystery? Who is the person buried in it? How did he live? This book tries to solve the mystery of persons living in colonial America, hundreds of years ago. By examining the bones, we discover whether the person is wealthy or poor, male or female. On one dig, anthropologists discovered a murdered young adult!

Note: The author was able to view the bones of colonial Americans who lived between 1600 and 1700 as a forensic anthropologist unearthed them. Some bones were revealed to be from aristocrats like Sir Lionel Copley, the first royal governor of Maryland. Other bones were of a teenage boy who was probably an indentured servant and who could have been murdered by his master. The book uses photographs, sidebars, and diagrams to explain the mysteries of life—and death. Out of respect for the culture, no Native American graves were unearthed.

Watanabe, Ken. *Problem Solving 101: A Simple Book for Smart People*. New York: Penguin, 2009. Ages 9+.

Nonfiction.

Related books: *Become a Problem Solving Genius* by Edward Zaccaro; *The Thinker's Toolkit* by Morgan D. Jones; *The Back of the Napkin: Solving Problems and Selling Ideas with Pictures* by Dan Roam.

Booktalk: Do you have a problem? Everybody does, you know. Once you read this book, you will never worry about solving problems. Instead, you'll approach all your problems with insight and skill. So hurry, hurry, hurry! Sign up for the class, *Problem Solving 101*!

Note: First published in Japan in 2007, this book provides practical tips for problem solving. The author introduces cartoon characters like the Mushroom Lovers, a band that needs to find an audience, along with John the Octopus, who wants to become a famous animator and director. The illustrations by Alan Sanders are a bit childlike, but the approach is fun and useful for all ages.

BOOKTALKS

Teens

Ackroyd, Peter. *Poe: A Life Cut Short*. **Ackroyd's Brief Lives. New York: Doubleday, 2008. Ages 13+.**

Biography.

Related Books: *In the Shadow of the Master* by Michael Connelly, ed.; *Lives of the Writers* by Kathleen Krull; poetry and short stories by Edgar Allan Poe.

Booktalk: "I could not love except where Death/Was mingling his wish with Beauty's breath." Edgar Allan Poe wrote this poem before he was 20. What attracted him to death at such an early age? Maybe the reason is that he was an orphan and lost everyone he loved, including his wife, his 13-year-old cousin. He was both afraid of and intrigued by death. And that's why he is the Master of Horror.

Note: Edgar Allan Poe (1809–1849) lived a life that was full of sadness and tragedy. His mother and father died early; he lost his adopted mother. Later, he also lost his young wife (a cousin whom he married when she was 13 years old). Biographers still aren't certain how he died since he was wearing strange clothes in a bar. Maybe he was being paid to vote since the bar was also a polling location. Even though this book has few photographs, young people will find his tragic life fascinating.

Anderson, Laurie Halse. *Wintergirls*. **New York: Viking, 2009. Ages 13+.**

Realistic fiction.

Related books: *If I Stay* by Gayle Forman; *Looks* by Madeline George; *Thirteen Reasons Why* by Jay Asher.

Booktalk: Cassie's dead. She called me 33 times. I didn't answer. She was a Wintergirl, just like I am, with a matchstick body. Boys call me Dead Girl Walking. I guess they're right. If I keep on going this way—thin, thinner, thinnest—I'll just disappear. Maybe I'll freeze to death, just like Cassie, and become a ghost.

Note: The main character, Lia, has anorexia nervosa and cuts herself, but she also suffers from depression and guilt. Her friend Cassie suffered from bulimia before her death. The author uses Lia's diary to great effect, with strike-through sentences, repetition, and even blank pages. Lia counts every calorie as her mind unravels from lack of food. This could be used as a group-read with older girls, but be aware of mild profanity.

Austen, Jane, and Seth Grahame-Smith. *Pride and Prejudice and Zombies*. **Philadelphia, PA: Quirk, 2009. Ages 15+.**

Horror; romance.

Related books: *The Zombie Survival Guide* by Max Brooks; *Zombie Blondes* by Brian James; *War of the Worlds with Blood, Guts and Zombies* by H. G. Wells and Eric S. Brown.

Booktalk: "It is a truth universally acknowledged that a zombie in possession of brains must be in want of more brains." All you zombie lovers will eat up this book. You romance lovers will fall in love with this book. What are you waiting for?

Note: This book could lead to reading Jane Austen's classic *Pride and Prejudice* or horror classics. Why not have the book clubbers write and illustrate a horror satire on another classic?

Citro, Joseph A., Mark Moran, and Mark Sceurman, eds. *Weird New England: Your Travel Guide to New England's Local Legends and Best Kept Secrets*. **New York: Sterling, 2005. Ages 13+.**

Nonfiction; horror.

Related books: *Weird U.S.* by Mark Moran and Mark Sceurman; *Did Lizzie Borden Ax for It?* by David Rehak; *The Haunting of America* by William J. Birnes and Joel Martin.

Booktalk: Want to go traveling to one of the weirdest places on earth? Let's go to New England, the northern part of the United States. This is the land of witches, Frog People, and vampires. Find out all the strange urban legends of this cold country. Then go visit the haunted areas—if you dare!

Note: This highly recommended illustrated book contains fascinating stories about New England ghosts, ancient mysteries, bizarre beasts, and haunted cemeteries. You should only have to booktalk this book one time; the young adults will grab this one and keep it circulating.

De La Cruz, Melissa. *Girl Stays in the Picture: A Girl Novel*. **New York: Simon & Schuster, 2009. Ages 13+.**

Realistic fiction.

Related books: *The Summer I Turned Pretty* by Jenny Han; *Don't Judge a Girl by Her Cover* by Ally Carter; *The Sisterhood of the Traveling Pants* series by Ann Brashares.

Booktalk: What's it like being a teen superstar? Devon has the lead in a movie; she's a recording diva turned actress. She also had a drug problem. Her friend Livia has lost weight, and now she's beautiful. But Livia doesn't feel beautiful; she feels fat and ugly. Casey is an assistant to Summer, another teen superstar. The three girls become friends, and sparks begin to fly!

Note: A high-interest book about teens who are the Beautiful People in Saint Tropez, France. Devon has past drug problems and needs this movie role to reinvigorate her career. Livia becomes Devon's friend and supporter, even though her father is the producer of the movie. Casey is only an assistant, but her kindness draws Devon and Livia to her. Together they support one another through betrayals, paparazzi, and romance. Because of the cliffhanger ending, groups might want to continue this teen soap opera.

Dessen, Sarah. *Just Listen.* **New York: Penguin, 2006. Ages 15+.**

Realistic fiction.

Related books: *Speak* by Laurie Halse Anderson; *Trapped! Cages of Mind and Body* edited by Lois Duncan; *Lock and Key* by Sarah Dessen.

Booktalk: Annabel Greene is a young beautiful model who has it all. But does she? No one knows that she is hiding a deep, dark secret. Then she meets Owen. He hates secrets. He thinks keeping secrets is the same as a lie. Will Annabel be able to tell about that night when she and Sophie stopped being friends?

Note: Sarah Dessen writes books that discuss important issues for teens. This plot involves a sexual assault at a drunken teenage party. Annabel decides to remain silent so that she will not bother her troubled family. Her friend Owen, who has his own anger management issues, explains that ignoring troubling issues will destroy the soul.

Forman, Gayle. *If I Stay.* **New York: Dutton, 2009. Ages 13+.**

Realistic fiction.

Related books: *The Lovely Bones* by Alice Sebold; *Sisters in Sanity* by Gayle Forman; *Wintergirls* by Laura Halse Anderson.

Booktalk: Mia is responsible for killing her family in a horrific car accident. Now she is in a coma. Her mind is still active as she reflects on her life. Should she go or stay?

Note: This book is based on a real-life incident. Mia loves her hippie family, her music, and her boyfriend. All that is taken away when she is driving the car that leads to her family's death. This 196-page book is perfect for reluctant readers who like reading about death; the surprise is that this is a life-affirming book. Some profanity and a mild sexual scene occur.

George, Jessica Day. *Princess of the Midnight Ball.* **New York: Bloomsbury, 2009. Ages 13+.**

Fantasy.

Related books: *Beauty* by Robin McKinley; *Snow White and Rose Red* by Patricia Wrede; *Sun and Moon, Ice and Snow* by Jessica Day George.

Booktalk: Princess Rose and her 11 sisters are under a spell. They are condemned to dance each night for the wicked King Under Stone. Then Rose meets Galen, a handsome gardener. Through their love and their invisibility cloak, they will try to break the King's curse. Will they succeed?

Note: This novel is based on the Brothers Grimm's folktale "The Twelve Dancing Princesses." All the sisters are named after flowers and are spunky heroines. Galen, the gardener, enjoys knitting, and his magical knitting patterns contribute to the plot.

James, Brian. *Zombie Blondes*. New York: Feiwel, 2008. Ages 13+.

Horror.

Related books: *Unabridged, Unabashed and Undead: The Best Zombie Short Stories* by Eric S. Brown; *Living Dead: The Reaper's Reward* by Oliver Church; *Max Mooth: Cyber Sleuth and the Case of the Zombie Virus* by Stephen Kogan.

Booktalk: Hannah Sanders is the new girl in high school. She is attracted to the blonde cheerleaders who almost seem to be clones: all blonde whose names begin with the letter "M." She doesn't know they are zombies, but she's about to find out!

Note: This book does not pull any punches with its horror scenes (although the scenes are not graphic), and its cliffhanger ending is reminiscent of a *Twilight Zone* episode. Highly recommended as a horror book for young people who are not quite ready for Stephen King.

Meyer, Stephenie. *Twilight*. New York: Little Brown, 2005. Ages 13+.

Horror; romance.

Related books: *The Twilight Companion: The Unauthorized Guide to the Series* by Lois H. Gresh; *New Moon, Eclipse*, and *Breaking Dawn* by Stephenie Meyer; *Vampire Kisses* series by Ellen Schreiber; *Jessica's Dating on the Dark Side* by Beth Fantasky.

Booktalk: I fell in love with Edward at first sight. He was so pale, good looking, and mysterious. But slowly I learned he was a vampire. What's a girl to do? I'm hungry for his love, but he's hungry for my blood!

Note: Younger readers could also read this book because there is no sex or profanity, but make certain they can handle the subject matter.

Moore, Mary Tyler. *Growing Up Again: Life, Loves, and Oh Yeah, Diabetes*. New York: St. Martin, 2009. Ages 13+.

Biography; nonfiction.

Related books: *Needles* by Andie Dominick; *The Sun, the Rain, and the Insulin* by Joan Mac-Cracken; *When Diabetes Hits Home* by Wendy Satin Rapaport; *Sugar Was My Best Food* by Carol Antoinette Peacock.

Booktalk: Maybe you know Mary Tyler Moore from television. She starred on *The Mary Tyler Moore Show* and *The Dick Van Dyke Show*. But she is much more than an actress. Do you know she has type 1 diabetes, something she's had for 40 years? Here's her story and how she's coped with a life-threatening illness.

Note: This book provides valuable appendices with information about diabetes, drills, testing, complications, stem cells, and a resource guide. You can also use this as a biography or research book on diabetes.

Schwartz, Evan I. *Finding Oz: How L. Frank Baum Discovered the Great American Story.* **Boston, MA: Houghton, 2009. Ages 15+.**

Biography.

Related books: *The Wizard of Oz* series by L. Frank Baum; *The Annotated Wizard of Oz* by L. Frank Baum.

Booktalk: How did the author Frank Baum create the magical Land of Oz? From where did all his ideas come? Would you believe the Wicked Witch of the North was based on his mother-in-law? Did you know the Wizard was based on Thomas Edison and the circus conman on P. T. Barnum? And that the author didn't start writing the series until he was 44 years old?

Note: A fascinating look at Frank Baum, the author of the *Wizard of Oz* series, including his failed attempts as a chicken farmer, actor, and marketer of petroleum products. Instead, he put all of his failures into his 15-book series to create a magical Oz. His mother-in-law, Matilda Joslyn Gage, was a fascinating feminist, working with Susan B. Anthony and Elizabeth Cady Stanton. The author also links Baum's series to Theosophy, a mixture of neo-Platonism, Buddhism, and Hinduism.

Soto, Gary. *Partly Cloudy: Poems of Love and Longing.* **New York: Houghton, 2009. Ages 13+.**

Poetry; romance.

Related books: *A Lion's Hunger: Poems of First Love* by Ann Turner; *New and Selected Poems* by Gary Soto; poems by Emily Dickinson and Walt Whitman.

Booktalk: "Love is like the weather/Sometimes stormy/Sometimes sunny/Sometimes partly cloudy." These poems come from both sides: a girl's tears and a boy's body. Will their love survive the partly cloudy skies?

Note: In short poems of free verse, the author discusses first love, jealousy, rejection, and loneliness. The book is told from both a boy and a girl's perspective, making the book useable as Reader's Theater.

Steifvater, Maggie. *Lament: The Faerie Queen's Deception.* **Woodbury, MN: Flux, 2008. Ages 16+.**

Fantasy.

Related books: *Wicked Lovely, Ink Exchange* and *Fragile Eternity* by Alyson Noel; *Graceling* by Kristin Cashore.

Booktalk: Deirdre Monaghan is a 16-year-old music student. She meets Luke at a concert. Luke's intention is to murder her for the cruel Faerie Queen, but instead he falls in love with her. Now Deirdre knows that, if Luke can't kill her, it's the Faerie Queen's job. Will Deirdre escape her death?

Note: This book describes the Celtic faeries in folklore: mischievous, sometimes cruel creatures that prey on unprotected humans. Since this is more complex and violent than most fantasies (and includes some profanity), recommend this book only to mature readers.

Tyson, Neil DeGrasse. *The Pluto Files: The Rise and Fall of America's Favorite Planet*. New York: Norton, 2009. Ages 13+.

Nonfiction.

Related books: *Universe* by Martin Rees; *When Is a Planet Not a Planet? The Story of Pluto* by Elaine Scott; *The Book of Pluto* by Steven Forrest.

Booktalk: Before there was Pluto, there was Planet X. Planet X was discovered by a farm boy in 1930. Eventually the planet was named after Pluto, the Greek god of the dead and the underworld. But is Pluto really a planet? That's one of the many mysteries of Pluto.

Note: Fascinating, readable study of the discovery of Pluto. Throughout the book are cartoons and photographs, giving a light touch to the science of astronomy.

 From *Book Clubbing! Successful Book Clubs for Young People* by Carol Littlejohn. Santa Barbara, CA: Linworth. Copyright © 2011.

POSTER CONTEST

For All Ages

Colorful and catchy book posters can be mounted and displayed everywhere and used year after year. Sponsoring a poster contest will ensure that book posters will adorn your meeting space and school.

Poster Contest Rules: Consider using these rules for your poster contest:

✦ The sponsor selects a deadline date for all entries.

✦ Participants design a poster of their favorite book.

✦ Each poster contains the name of the book and author.

✦ The illustrator must sign each poster on the back with the name, date, and grade.

✦ Posters created by students must be their own original artwork. Copyrighted characters (such as Superman) or copyrighted clip art are not acceptable.

✦ The content of the poster graphically describes the book by theme, characters. or plot. Text can be added to describe the illustrations.

✦ Participants can enter the poster contest multiple times.

✦ Students may use a variety of materials, such as watercolor, pen and ink, crayon, chalk, and markers. Computer text can also be used sparingly.

✦ Entrants are encouraged to use recycled materials.

✦ Each poster should be easy to see and read.

✦ The size of each poster should be at least 8-1/2 inches by 11 inches. The maximum size for each poster is 18 inches by 24 inches.

✦ All entries must be accompanied by a written permission slip, stating that posters become the property of the organization and can be reproduced.

✦ All participants can receive a certificate of achievement.

✦ If the sponsor is awarding prizes, the prizes can be announced in advance.

Use of posters. If possible, all posters should be laminated. The best posters will be displayed first, but posters will be changed regularly so that all participants will have their work displayed. Attempt to place the appropriate book close to the poster.

Keyword search. For further information, try "poster contests for kids," "poster contests for high school students," "art contests for kids," and "art contests for high school students." For deadline contests that award money or prizes, place the current year after keyword search.

PUPPET SHOW

For Preteens and Teens

Younger ages love puppets. Use them anytime before, during, or after meetings. Use puppets to turn pages or to talk between stories. A puppet show is also a way for older readers to combine creativity, artistic talent, and showmanship. And, if the puppet show can be performed in front of a younger audience, this is a perfect way to advertise the book club to younger students who may want to join in the future.

History. Puppetry exists throughout all cultures and began at least 3,000 years ago. The puppets were generally small in size and manipulated by an unseen puppeteer behind a stage. Other facts about puppets include ("Puppet"):

✦ A *marionette* is moved by strings or wires from above and is usually controlled by experienced puppeteers.

✦ A *hand puppet* conceals the hand of the puppeteer beneath the costume; even young, inexperienced children can operate a hand puppet. These hand puppets can be made from socks, cloth, or foam.

✦ Other puppets are *stick puppets* that consist of a Popsicle stick glued to either a paper plate or construction paper.

Puppet show goals. This activity involves making puppets and performing a puppet show for a younger audience.

✦ The puppet show involves a workshop (two to four meetings) and the performance.

✦ Puppeteers need to be older because they must use sharp utensils.

✦ Ask each person to bring a pair of sharp scissors with his name on it, a sock (or whatever materials will make the puppet), and an audiocassette for recording the play.

✦ If the participant wants to perform in the show, she must attend all the sessions.

Preproduction

Planning the show takes time.

✦ **Finding resources.** Check the library for books on making puppets, designing a puppet stage, and selecting play by using Dewey number 791.5. Also, select a play for performing by searching Dewey numbers 398.2 (folktales and fairy tales) and 800 (literature and plays). Or just select your favorite picture books.

✦ **Can't find a play?** Consider writing your own play or try the rapping rhyme "Trip Trap Rap," described in this chapter under "Rapping Rhymes."

✦ **Audiotape the play.** If possible, create an audiotape of the play. Perhaps you could use various voices or sound effects. Make a copy of the tape for each puppeteer to take home and practice.

- **Making the puppets.** After discovering the play, decide what kind of puppets you plan to make with book clubbers. Younger ages can design "stick puppets" or "sock puppets." For safety reasons, only adults should operate hot-glue guns.

- **Choosing roles.** At the first meeting, book clubbers select roles for the puppet performance. The sponsor lists each part on a folded sheet of paper and asks students to draw their parts from a designated container. Members may exchange their character with another person if the person is agreeable.

- **Rehearsals.** Two meetings of three hours are scheduled for the workshop. The first meeting is for making puppets; the next meeting is for rehearsing the play. During rehearsals, the puppeteers should sit in chairs in a straight line across the stage so that the sponsor can direct the puppeteers. Encourage the puppeteers to choreograph the puppets, but the sponsor has the final word.

- **Behind the stage.** After finalizing choreography, move the puppeteers to their proper places behind the puppet stage. (For comfort, puppeteers can use kneepads.) Check the sound system. If possible, videotape the rehearsal so that puppeteers can visually see and correct their mistakes.

Performance Day

- **No performance fees.** Remember, for copyright issues, none of these shows can be performed for a fee.

- **Videotape the performance.** Arrange for someone to record the puppet show as a lasting memory.

- **The audience.** Invite parents and preschoolers to the puppet show. Play the prerecorded script during the performance so that the puppeteers can concentrate on their puppets.

- **Take a final bow!** Have the puppeteers to take a bow with their puppets at the end of the show.

- **Final prize.** All puppeteers will keep their puppets.

Dewey number. Use 791.53 for more books on making and performing with puppets.

Keyword search. Try "puppetry," "puppet," and "puppeteer" for current books and Web sites.

Works Cited on "Puppet Show"

Littlejohn, Carol. *Puppet Workshop Series*. Pittsburgh: n.p., Feb. 1991. Print.
    Two-page handout for librarians distributed during a presentation at a Carnegie Library workshop.

"Puppet." *Wikipedia*. Web. 11 June 2010.
    Useful information about the history and uses of puppetry.

RAPPING RHYMES

For All Ages

Rapping Rhymes are poems delivered in a singsong voice. These rhymes are recited to younger readers; older readers can write their own rhymes. "Trip Trap Rap" is based on the Norwegian folktale "The Three Billy Goats Gruff."

Trip Trap Rap

By
Carol Littlejohn

Once upon a time by the edge of a bluff
Lived three billy goats with the last name Gruff.
They liked crunching and munching on the thick green grass,
But a big ugly troll wouldn't let them pass.

There was a bridge these goats had to cross
Guarded by a dude who thought he was boss.
The first billy goat was so little and small;
He hardly had any meat on him at all.

The goat stepped on the bridge—trip, trapping on each hoof,
And the troll heard the trip trapping on his roof:
'WHO'S THAT TRIP, TRAP, TRIP, TRAP, TRAPPING?
WHO DISTURBS ME WHILE I'M NAPPING?"

"I'm just a kid; I got no meat on my bones,
But someone's coming who is halfway grown.
Wait for my brother; he's much bigger than I.
As goats go, he's a regular guy."

"BE OFF WITH YOU! YOU'RE SO SKINNY AND SMALL!
ONE BITE, CHEW, SWALLOW—AND YOU'RE GONE, THAT'S
ALL!
GO EAT THAT THICK, GREEN GRASS
SO YOU'LL BE FATTER WHEN YOU COME BACK TO PASS!"

(Trip trap trip trap trip trap trap)

Next came the goat that was medium in size,
One of those just plain ordinary guys.
He eyed that bully hiding near the bridge,
Blocking that thick green grass on the ridge.

He stepped on the bridge—trip, trapping on each hoof,
And the troll heard the trip, trapping on his roof:
'WHO'S THAT TRIP, TRAP, TRIP, TRAP TRAPPING?
WHO DISTURBS ME WHILE I'M NAPPING?"

"I'm just an average guy, but take my advice:
I'm not the sort of goat you should look at twice. Wait
for my brother; he's much bigger than I.
And while you're waiting, I will say goodbye!"

(Trip trap trip trap trip trap trap)

Next came the ba-a-adest billy goat of all.
He had whipped Godzilla, King Kong, and the Claw!
He stepped on the bridge—TRIP, TRAPPING on each hoof,
And the troll heard the TRIP, TRAPPING on his roof.

"WHO'S THAT TRIP, TRAP, TRIP, TRAP, TRAPPING?
WHO DISTURBS ME WHILE I'M NAPPING?"
"IT IS I, THE BA-A-ADEST BILLY GOAT YOU'LL MEET.
I'LL KNOCK YOUR BLOCK OFF AND YOU AIN'T A STREET!"

Then the ba-a-adest billy goat lowered his horns
And knocked that troll back to where he was born.
The troll was gone, gone for good, my friend.
And like all kids' tales, this must come to an end.

Trip! Trap!
End of rap!

Revised version, copyright 2009 by Carol Littlejohn.
Other versions were published in Storytelling World
(Winter 1993: 14) and Storytelling (May/June 1995: 14-15).

"TRIP TRAP RAP" OR "THE THREE BILLY GOATS GRUFF" ACTIVITIES

For Younger Readers (Ages 3–8)

Finger plays. Using your left arm as the bridge, place your right fist as the troll directly under the bridge (left arm). Use the small finger for the small goat and the index finger for the medium-sized goat. The ba-a-adest billy goat is performed with the right forearm, which knocks the troll off the bridge. To get into the singsong beat, begin by snapping your fingers and end with a finger snap.

Read-aloud. Read the rap at the beginning of a meeting and discuss the themes, while presenting other versions of "The Three Billy Goats Gruff." If you are a librarian, make these tapes and books available for checkout.

Puppet show or flannel-board presentation. After the rap, you can use flannel-board pieces or puppets to act out the story.

Gross motor activities. Children act out the story with chairs or a table covered with a blanket. Assign the troll role and the three goats.

Language. Categorizing by size: small, medium, and large.

Recipe. Use these ingredients to create a visual presentation while telling the story (Carpenter):

> Chunky peanut butter for the dirt
>
> Coconut dyed green for the grass
>
> Large Corn Chip for the bridge
>
> Three white marshmallows (mini for the small goat)
>
> Purple grape for the Troll
>
> Blue Fruit Rollup for the stream

Discussion questions. Depending on the age of the group members, discussion questions can range from size categorization to themes of good against evil. In many ways, this Norwegian folktale describes a classic bullying situation. Some questions that can be discussed:

◆ What is a bully? (*"Trip Trap Rap" uses the word "bully" deliberately. The problem of bullying should be discussed so that even the youngest children are aware how a bully threatens their well-being.*)

◆ Is the troll a bully? (*The troll is threatening three goats, insisting that he will eat them, but he seems more nasty than hungry. Most bullies are angry for many reasons.*)

◆ How do the first two goats get across the bridge? (*By using their wits, not their size.*)

◆ Is the last goat a bully, too? (*This question should stir up some interesting answers among older students. After all, the last bully goat uses violence instead of his wits. Is the largest goat a protector or just another bully? Another perspective is that the protagonist is the troll who misses an opportunity to accept a good deal rather than greedily waiting for a spectacular meal.)*

✦ Most important, what will you do if a bully bothers you or someone else? (*Tell a trusted adult, including teachers, parents, and relatives. If you have friends, tell them, as well. Don't be quiet and suffer needlessly.*)

Preteens and Teens

Read-aloud. Reading a rap can inspire other students to write one of their own. Explain that the folktale is in public domain—no copyright issues—and has many interpretations and variations.

For example, in 2008, the British Broadcasting Corporation (BBC) adapted the folktale with the troll as a tragic victim. How does that approach change the story? How would students change the story to reflect the current times? Encourage writing variations of the folktale or any other folktales that interest them. (Acquire written permission before displaying or cataloging any projects. Refer to the back of the book for a permission form.)

Reader's Theater. Using five characters from the story (narrator, troll, and three billy goats), book clubbers can read the parts, using appropriate voices.

Puppet show. The group can make puppets of the goats and troll to perform behind a puppet stage. Prerecord the script so the students can concentrate on their handmade puppets.

BOOKS ABOUT CONFLICT RESOLUTION

Preteens

Estes, Eleanor, and Louis Slobodkin, ill. *The Hundred Dresses*. New York: Sandpiper, 2004. Ages 8–12.

Fiction.

Booktalk: Peggy knew that Wanda Petronski didn't have 100 dresses as she claimed. Wanda was too poor to own 100 dresses. She always wore the same faded blue dress. So what was wrong with making fun of a girl who is a liar?

Note: This 1944 Newbery winner never dates. A great read-aloud for younger readers. If you use this for a group-read, try *A Guide for Using Hundred Dresses for the Classroom*.

Hale, Shannon, and Dale Hale; Nathan Hale, ill. *Rapunzel's Revenge*. New York: Bloomsbury USA, 2008. Ages 9–12.

Graphic novel.

Booktalk: I guess you know the story about Rapunzel letting down her hair and marrying a prince. But what if Rapunzel meets Jack the Beanstalk? Try this comic book for a twisted tale of adventure.

Note: This should be a popular addition to the library with its color graphics, hair-raising adventures, and strong female character. Of course, it ends happily as most folktales do. Recommend this for middle school students because of the word "pregnant," but, if this is no problem, add this one to younger library collections.

Sacher, Louis. *Holes*. New York: Farrar, 2008. Print. Ages 9–12.

Realistic fiction.

Booktalk: Does digging a hole make a bad boy a good person? Stanley Yelnats is sent to Camp Green Lake instead of jail. He meets a gang of other "bad boys" who spend all day digging a five-foot hole. Stanley doesn't know that digging holes will change his bad luck to good.

Note: This 1994 Newbery winner is a comic blend of mystery and drama. A great read-aloud for younger readers. Consider using *A Guide for Using* Holes *for the Classroom*. If possible, show the 2003 movie *Holes*.

 From *Book Clubbing! Successful Book Clubs for Young People* by Carol Littlejohn. Santa Barbara, CA: Linworth. Copyright © 2011.

Stolz, Mary. *The Bully of Barkham Street*. **New York: HarperCollins, 1987. Ages 9–12.**

Realistic fiction.

Booktalk: It's easy to hate Marvin. Marvin is a bully. His neighbor Edward hates him and thinks everybody should hate Marvin. Edward doesn't know the whole story. Once you know Marvin, it's not so easy to hate him.

Note: This 1964 book still resonates because, unfortunately, bullies are still in schools. Marvin has many home problems and feels inadequate. An earlier book, *A Dog on Barkham Street* (1960), tells Edward's side of the story.

BOOKS ABOUT CONFLICT RESOLUTION

Teens

George, Madeleine. *Looks.* **New York: Viking, 2008. Ages 13+.**

Realistic fiction.

Booktalk: Have you ever wanted revenge? What if someone at school makes fun of you? What if a friend betrays your trust? Meghan Ball is obese; Aimee Zorn is anorexic. They don't seem likely friends. And they aren't friends until a popular girl and boy belittle them. Now they want revenge.

Note: This open-ended novel is one of the best books about conflict resolution because it also covers eating disorders, family dysfunctions, and school cliques. Meghan has been friends with Cara Roy since grade school, but, when Meghan gains weight, Cara drops their friendship. Aimee Zorn is the anorexic new girl who is a poet. When Cara plagiarizes Aimee's poem, Aimee wants revenge. Meghan and Aimee plot to humiliate Cara and the basketball star and bully J-Bar. Also highly recommended as a group-read because of the probing questions it poses (without offering glib answers).

Hicks, Faith Erin. *The War at Ellsmere.* **San Jose, CA: SLG, 2008. Ages 11–18.**

Graphic novel.

Booktalk: Jun thinks going to a private boarding school on scholarship is an opportunity of a lifetime. Instead, she must face the bully of the school, Emily, who has it in for Jun. At first, Jun uses her words to fight back, but sometimes Emily just goes too far.

Note: This manga art style will be especially inviting to reluctant readers. *Zombies Calling* creator Faith Erin Hicks tells a compelling story of how two girls (Jun and her best friend, Cassie) find a way to resolve the problem of a bully who has the support of parents and school administrators.

Patterson, James, and Leopoldo Gout. Art by Klaus Lyngeled, Jon Girin, and Joseph McLamb. *Daniel X: Alien Hunter.* **New York: Little, Brown, 2008. Ages 13+.**

Graphic novel.

Booktalk: Daniel X is an alien who can shape-change and can see his long-dead parents. Then he runs up against the evil Number 7. Number 7 can also shape-shift and perform all kinds of destructive tricks. Who will win the challenge?

Note: The color illustrations are impressive, although the story can be confusing. Daniel X makes friends with his archenemy's son, Kildare. It ends with a Buddhist parable in a science fiction context. Because of the graphics, highly recommended for reluctant readers.

Van Diepen, Allison. *Snitch*. New York: Simon Pulse, 2007. Ages 14+.

Realistic fiction.

Booktalk: South Bay High School has its gangs, and no one crosses the line without injury. So Julia DiVino and her best friend Q stay out of the way of the Crips and the Bloods. Then Julia meets the new guy, Eric. He decides to join the Crips. Now Julia must decide. Should she join the Crips or be a snitch?

Note: This pistol-packing drama contains profanity and ethnic slurs that are totally realistic to the plot. When Julia snitches on her boyfriend Eric, she is beaten by her gang. Later, she discovers that Eric is himself a snitch, trying to infiltrate the Crips for the police.

Williams-Garcia, Rita. *Jumped*. New York: Harper Teen, 2009. Ages 14+.

Realistic fiction.

Booktalk: The word is buzzing all over school. Girl fight! Pass it on! Girl fight! When? Fight starts after school!

Trina keeps getting in Dominique's space. Of course, Dominique has to get revenge. Trina doesn't even know Dominique is mad. Only Leticia knows. Should she tell?

Note: This short novel takes place during one school day. Dominique is mad because poor grades prevent her from playing basketball. She turns her anger on Trina, who doesn't even know she's upset Dominique. Leticia knows about the upcoming fight but doesn't tell anyone in authority—or even Trina. So Trina goes to the hospital and Dominique goes to jail. Some mild profanity, but the book is unforgettable and, unfortunately, all too realistic.

Works Cited on "Rapping Rhymes"

Carpenter, Kathleen. "#1948. Activities to Accompany *The Three Billy Goats Gruff.*" *Early Childhood Chatboard.* Web. 2 June 2009.

> Try these activities with younger children after reading or telling the rap.

Littlejohn, Carol. "Trip Trap Rap." Home page. Web. 18 June 2010. www.carollittlejohn.com.

> Rapping rhyme is available online.

Littlejohn, Carol. "Trip Trap Rap: A Rappin' Rhyme." *Storytelling World* Winter/Spring 1993: 14. Print.

> Contains "Trip Trap Rap" rapping rhyme with some slight changes.

Littlejohn, Carol. "Writing the Rappin' Rhyme." *Storytelling Magazine* Mar. 1995: 14–15. Print.

> Describes how to write a rapping rhyme.

Russell, Cheryl. *A Guide for Using* The Hundred Dresses *for the Classroom.* Santa Barbara, CA: Teacher Created, 2004. Print.

> Guide to the Newbery winner *The Hundred Dresses* by Eleanor Estes.

Zampino, Belina, and Rebecca Clark. *A Guide for Using* Holes *for the Classroom.* Santa Barbara, CA: Teacher Created, 2004. Print.

> Guide to the Newbery winner *Holes* by Louis Sachar.

READ-ALOUD BOOKS

For Ages 3–8

Books can be read aloud to children of any age, but this activity is devoted to beginning readers. For read-aloud recommendation for all ages, check this Web site by Jim Trelease: www.trelease-on-reading.com.

Format. After each suggested title, a booktalk, related books, and note are provided. As a reminder, a *booktalk* is written only to provide a brief introduction to the book. After the booktalk, begin reading the book aloud. Point out the illustrations and explain any unfamiliar words. Interactively share the book with children. *Related books* provide several reading suggestions. The *note* offers more information on the book with suggestions for reading activities.

Agee, Jon. *Orangutan Tongs: Poems to Tangle Your Tongue*. **New York: Hyperion, 2009. Ages 5–8.**

Read-aloud.

Related books: *A Twister of Twists, A Tangler of Tongues* by Alvin Schwartz; *A Foot in the Mouth* by Paul B. Janezcko and Chris Raschka; *Go Hang a Salami! I'm a Lasagna Hog* by Jon Agee.

Booktalk: Anyone know what a tongue twister is? That's a phrase that makes your tongue get twisted when you say words very fast, so fast that it comes out sounding like—well, nonsense. By the way, can you say "tongue twister" five times very fast?

Note: Tongue twisters are used by speech pathologists to help children enunciate. More tongue twisters are available at the Web site www.indianchild.com/tongue_twisters.htm.

Auch, Mary Jane, and Herm Auch, ill. *The Plot Chickens*. **New York: Holiday, 2009. Ages 5–8.**

Read-aloud.

Related books: *Author: A True Story* by Helen Lester; *What Do Authors Do?* by Ellen Christelow; *Aunt Isabel Tells a Good One* by Kate Duke.

Booktalk: Henrietta the chicken loves to read, so she decides to write a book. First, she reads a book, *Writing Rules!* by Reed Moore. Once she learns all the rules, she starts to write her book, *The Perils of Maxine*. It's an eggs-traodinary book!

Note: The author explains the rules of writing a book: invent a main character, "hatch" a plot, develop the plot, give main character a problem, build suspense, write story by using all five senses, and, finally, resolve the problem. Adults can help children write and illustrate a story, using these rules.

Aylesworth, Jim, and Barbara McClintock, ill. *Our Abe Lincoln: An Old Tune with New Lyrics*. **New York: Scholastic, 2009. Ages 5–9.**

Read-aloud.

Related books: *Abe Lincoln Crosses a Creek* by Deborah Hopkinson and John Hendrix; *Mr. Lincoln's Whiskers* by Karen B. Winnick; *Abe Lincoln: The Boy Who Loved Books* by Kay Winters and Nancy Carpenter.

Booktalk: Abraham Lincoln was president of the United States 150 years ago. During that time, a song was sung about Abe Lincoln that is a great sing-along. So get your voices ready to sing about our Abe Lincoln!

Note: The traditional folk song is based on the tune of "The Old Grey Mare." The colorful illustrations conclude with children presenting a play about Abe Lincoln. An author's note explains each page. Children could perform creative dramatics by acting the song.

Bishop, Nic. *Frogs*. New York: Scholastic Nonfiction, 2008. Ages 6+.

Nonfiction.

Related books: *Butterflies and Moths* by Nic Bishop; *Crocodile Safari* by Jim Arnosky; *Slither and Crawl: Eye to Eye with Reptiles* by Jim Arnosky.

Booktalk: Did you know that frogs are found on every continent except Antarctica? Almost all frogs have long back legs, large heads, big eyes, damp skin, and no tail. That's just many of the fascinating facts about frogs noted by Nic Bishop.

Note: The color photography encourages younger children to "read" the book, just as in all of Nic Bishop's books. For online printable worksheets and reading activities, try "frog activities for kindergarten."

Davis, Jacqueline, and S. D. Schindler, ill. *Tricking the Tallyman*. New York: Knopf, 2009. Ages 7+.

Read-aloud.

Related books: If You Lived in Colonial Times by Ann McGovern and June Otani; *Colonial Voices* by Kay Winters and Larry Day; *Welcome to Felicity's World, 1774* by Camela DeCaire and Jodi Evert.

Booktalk: Phineas Bump came to a small town many, many years ago to do one thing. He needed to find out exactly how many people live in this town. The U.S. government sent him on this journey. But no one trusts him. Find out how he tricks the townspeople to get those numbers he needs!

Note: In 1790, the first U.S. census was taken, and many people were suspicious of the government's demand for their personal information. They thought they would have to pay more taxes. Actually, the U.S. government needed these numbers to figure out how many Representatives each state would send to the House of Representatives. Sadly, in 1790, the Native Americans were not counted at all, and each slave was counted as three-fifths of a person. The text has a humorous story but includes an author's note to explain the census process. For an activity, try taking a brief census of the group (for gender and age).

dePaola, Tomie. *The Song of Francis*. New York: Putnam, 2009. Ages 5–8.

Read-aloud.

Related books: *Francis: The Poor Man of Assisi* by Tomie dePaola; *Miss Rumphius* by Barbara Cooney; *Owl Moon* by Jane Yolen.

Booktalk: Many years ago (more than 1,000 years ago!) there lived a poor man who loved animals. His name was St. Francis. St. Francis especially loved the birds. He thought the song of the birds spoke of God's love. What did the birds sing? Love, love, love.

Note: The author's tropical-hued collages tell the story of St. Francis's love of birds and animals. The only disappointment is that there is no author's note about St. Francis's life. St. Francis of Assisi (1181/1182–1226) is known as the patron saint of animals, Italy, and the environment. Many Catholic churches celebrate St. Francis's feast day on October 4 to honor animals. However, this celebration of birds and ecology is appropriate for any occasion. For activities, children can create bird collages from pre-cut construction paper.

Emberley, Rebecca, and Ed Emberley, ill. *Chicken Little*. **New York: Roaring Brooks, 2009. Ages 5–7.**

Read-aloud.

Related books: *Chicken Little* by Stephen Kellogg; *Henny Penny* by Paul Galdone; *The Gingerbread Boy* by Paul Galdone.

Booktalk: "The sky is falling! The sky is falling!" Who says? Chicken Little!

Note: This classic folktale is retold with a twist—the fox has allergies! The humorous drawings add to the frantic hustling of the animals that believe the sky is falling. For online printable coloring pages of *Chicken Little*, search "Chicken Little coloring page."

Florian, Douglas. *Dinothesaurs: Prehistoric Poems and Paintings*. **New York: Atheneum, 2009. Ages 7+.**

Read-aloud.

Related books: *Digging for Dinosaurs* by Aliki; *Ice Age* by DK Publishing; *Giant Sea Reptiles of the Dinosaur Age* by Caroline Arnold.

Booktalk: Who likes dinosaurs? Maybe you wouldn't want to meet one, but most of us love to learn about dinosaurs. Want to learn more? Then listen closely....

Note: Bold illustrations were created on a paper bag with a variety of materials, providing an entertaining collage. Humorous text provides a playful look at each type of dinosaur with helpful pronunciations. Includes glossary, list of dinosaur museums, and fossil sites. Could also be useful for all types of older readers, especially reluctant readers. For online dinosaur activities and coloring pages, try searching "dinosaur games."

French, Jackie, and Bruce Whatley, ill. *Diary of a Wombat*. **New York: Clarion, 2003. Ages 3–7.**

Read-aloud.

Related books: *How to Scratch a Wombat* by Jackie French and Bruce Whatley; *Koala Lou* by Mem Fox and Pamela Lofts; *Australia ABCs* by Sarah Heiman and Arturo Avila; *Bilby Moon* by Margaret Spurling.

Booktalk: This is the story of a lazy wombat. A wombat lives in Australia and looks a little like a bear. He loves to dig, eat, and sleep. So what is the story? Digging, eating, and sleeping, of course!

Note: This book is particularly useful for students doing projects on Australia or unusual animals. For facts, pictures, and activities with wombats, try this Web site: www.wombania.com.

Gerstein, Mordicai. *A Book.* **New York: Roaring Brook, 2009. Ages 6–8.**

Read-aloud.

Related books: *Library Mouse* by Daniel Kirk; *The House in the Night* by Susan Marie Swanson; *The Plot Chickens* by Mary Jane and Herm Auch.

Booktalk: What would it be like to live inside a book? One family lives inside a book, and all members of the family have a story. Father is a clown. Mother is a fire fighter. But the girl wants to tell her own story. What is her story?

Note: A girl goes in search of a story, meeting Mother Goose, fairy tale characters, pirates, astronauts, Alice in Wonderland, and a detective. Humorous dialogue with a comic-book flavor adds to the story. Ask children to draw themselves as adults. What will they be wearing or doing?

Gravett, Emily. *The Odd Egg.* **New York: Simon & Schuster, 2009. Ages 3–6.**

Read-aloud.

Related books: *Horton Hatches the Egg* by Dr. Seuss; *Are You My Mother?* by P. D. Eastmen; *The Extraordinary Egg* by Leo Lionni; *One Little Odd Egg* by Chris MacNeil.

Booktalk: All the animals have laid eggs except for Duck. Duck finally finds an egg and decides that this egg will be her egg. But what a surprise she gets when the egg hatches!

Note: Cleverly designed with graduated cut pages so that the egg grows larger and larger until out comes an alligator! For an egg unit that includes many activities for young children, use the Web site www.prekinders.com.

Hopkins, Lee Bennett, ed., and Julia Sarcone-Roach, ill. *Incredible Inventions.* **New York: Greenwillow, 2009. Ages 7+.**

Read-aloud.

Related books: *Spectacular Science: A Book of Poems* by Lee Bennett Hopkins and Virginia Halstead; *The Adventures of a Plastic Bottle* by Alison Inches and Pete Whitehead; *A Foot in the Mouth* by Paul Janeczko and Chris Raschko.

Booktalk: What is an invention? An invention is something that someone has created. For example, some inventions are blue jeans, the roller coaster, the Ferris wheel, and the Popsicle. Poetry is also an invention. Let's listen to these poems about inventions created by poets.

Note: These poems vary from couplets, free verse, and concrete poetry to haikus. At the end of the book is a detailed history (with a timeline) of the inventions of jigsaw puzzles, drinking straws, crayons, and escalators. Older children will enjoy this book because of its multiple reading interests: arts and crafts, science, history, and poetry. Children can make a craft from Popsicle sticks; use the online search "popsicle sticks crafts for kids."

Isadora, Rachel. *Rapunzel*. New York: Putnam, 2008. Ages 6–8.

Read-aloud.

Related books: *Rapunzel* by Paul O. Zelinsky and the Brothers Grimm; *Rapunzel* by Catherine McCafferty; *Rapunzel* by Dorothee Duntze.

Booktalk: This is an old story, told long before your parents or grandparents were born. This is the story of Rapunzel. Rapunzel is the name of a plant and, also, of a young girl. Rapunzel lives in Africa. Let's listen to her story.

Note: The rich collages are double-paged images that use broad strokes with burnt orange colors. The word "sorceress" may be unfamiliar to children, so either explain the word or substitute the word "witch." Rapunzel becomes pregnant by the prince, but this fact is never mentioned, only illustrated. Try to show different picture books of Rapunzel so that children learn that the story is told many different ways by different cultures. For free printable Rapunzel activities, try the Web site www.printactivities.com.

Ives, Penny. *Celestine: Drama Queen*. New York: Scholastic, 2009. Ages 5–8.

Read-aloud.

Related books: *Fancy Nancy: The Show Must Go On* by Jane O'Connor et al.; *Pinkalious* by Victoria Kann; *Katy Duck, Center Stage* by Alyssa Satin Capucilli and Harry Cole.

Booktalk: From the day Celestine danced out of her shell, she knew she would be a star. It was no surprise to her that she had a part in the school play. Of course she would be great—or would she?

Note: Celestine is a drama queen duck that wears pink clothing with a tiara. She just assumes she will be the star of the school play, but instead she gets a case of stage fright. Somehow she manages to do a quick dance and exits the stage. Her parents assure her that she'll always be a star. After the story, play "Duck, duck, goose," a traditional children's game for four or more players. The "fox" picks a "goose" within the circle by tapping him on the shoulder and then chasing "the goose" around the circle. As in Musical Chairs, the child without a seat or spot within the circle will be the next "fox."

Kimmel, Eric A., and Valeria Docampo, ill. *The Three Little Tamales*. Tarrytown, NY: Marshall Cavendish, 2009. Ages 5–8.

Read-aloud.

Related books: *The Runaway Tortilla* by Eric A. Kimmel; *The Gingerbread Cowboy* by Janet Squire and Holly Berry; *The True Story of the Three Little Pigs* by Jon Schieszka and Lane Smith; *The Stinky Cheese Man and Other Fairly Stinky Tales* by Jon Schieszka and Lane Smith.

Booktalk: How many children know the story "The Three Little Pigs"? Well, this story is slightly different—with a Mexican twist!

Note: Humorous story with colorful illustrations of three tamales that run away because they are afraid to be eaten. Unfortunately, they end up being pursued by a *lobo* (wolf) that plans to make them his dinner. The glossary and pronunciation guide at the beginning could be used as a Spanish lesson. After reading the story, ask children about other similar folktales ("The Three Little Pigs" and "The Gingerbread Boy"). Serving tamales can complete the activity.

Neuschwander, Cindy, Lisa Woodruff, ill., and Marilyn Burns. *Amanda Bean's Amazing Dream*. A Marilyn Burns Brainy Day Book. New York: Scholastic, 1998. Ages 5–8.

Read-aloud.

Related books: *The Greedy Triangle* by Marilyn Burns and Gordon Silveria; *Spaghetti and Meatballs for All!* by Marilyn Burns; *Math Patterns and Puzzles for Kids, Grades 2–4* by Kristy Fulton.

Booktalk: Meet Amanda Bean. She loves mathematics. But she doesn't know why she should learn to multiply numbers. Learn why as you travel into *Amanda Bean's Amazing Dream*.

Note: Provides helpful suggestions for parents and teachers, including extended children's learning activities.

Staines, Bill, and Kadir Nelson, ill. *All God's Critters*. New York: Simon & Schuster, 2009. Ages 3–8.

Read-aloud.

Related books: *We're Going on a Bear Hunt* by Michael Rosen and Helen Oxenbury; *Chicka Chicka Boom Boom* by Bill Martin Jr. et al.; *Brown Bear, Brown Bear, What Do You See?* by Bill Martin Jr. and Eric Carle.

Booktalk: All God's critters have a place in the choir! Join in with me because everyone has a part!

Note: Children can participate by imitating talking (low, high, loud), clapping, and imitating animal sounds. Music and lyrics are supplied at book's conclusion. Consider using Peter, Paul and Mary's version of the song from *In Their Times* album, available for download from Amazon and ITunes.

READER'S THEATER AND URBAN LEGENDS

For All Readers

Reader's Theater is spelled different ways: "reader's theater," "readers' theater," "readers' theatre," "readers theatre," "readers theater," and "reader's theatre." Occasionally, the activity is shortened to "RT." Regardless of the spelling, this activity involves reading aloud while seated. No costumes or props are required. Obviously, the group must be able to read the scripts, but readers of all ages can participate. For more details, read the teaching strategies listed under the appropriate age group.

Urban legends. Reader's Theater can be on any topic that interests book clubbers. The following RT script focuses on urban legends, since this topic seems to fascinate preteens and teens. *Urban legends* comprises modern folklore that is told as fact but that consists of fictional stories of horrific proportions. Urban legends exist in every country and language. Each story reveals the subconscious fears of its tellers: racism, crime, murder, and ghosts.

RT script. In the script *Too Good to Be True*, each reader tells an urban legend, and the rest of the members contribute to the chorus. If there aren't enough urban legends for your group, ask them to add to the RT script with other urban legends.

"Too Good to Be True!" Reader's Theater Script

Urban Legends: By Carol Littlejohn

Characters

Each reader reads one urban legend.

Chorus of readers

Play

Reader #1: Want to hear a story too good to be true? This happened to a friend of a friend. He is driving alone one night when he sees a beautiful girl. Who is she? He has never seen her before. He stops the car and offers her a ride. She tells him that she lives in the gray house outside town. Then she looks straight ahead, never speaking. When he arrives at her house, he notices that she has disappeared. Where is she? When he knocks on the door, he meets an old couple. They tell him that their daughter was killed on that same road more than 20 years ago. And tonight was her birthday!

Chorus: That's too good to be true!

Reader #2: Listen to this. Here's another ghost story. These two guys are driving to the high school prom. They see a beautiful girl they've never seen before. They invite her to the prom. She dances with them all night, but, whenever they touch her, she is deadly cold. While driving her home, they give her a jacket to keep her warm. When they drive back the next day to retrieve the jacket, they meet the girl's mother. She tells them her daughter died 10 years ago. She offers to show them her daughter's grave in the back yard. Guess what is on top of the grave? The jacket!

Chorus: That's too good to be true!

Reader #3: What about this one? My cousin says he heard about this girl attacked at the mall. The weird thing is that she was attacked as she was leaving the mall. Someone was under her car with a knife to slash her ankles and take her shoes!

Chorus: That's too good to be true!

Reader #4: Let's tell some animal urban legends. Once there was a lady who received a poodle for a birthday present. When her guests leave, she decides to give the dog a bath. All her towels are dirty, so she gets a bright idea. She decides to dry the dog by putting him in a microwave!

Chorus: That's too good to be true!

Reader #5: What about the choking Doberman? This lady owns a large Doberman dog. One day she comes home to discover the dog is choking. The lady takes and leaves the dog with the veterinarian. At home, she gets a call from the vet. He tells her to leave her house immediately. Inside the dog's throat were two human fingers! It turns out that a thief was hiding in her closet!

Chorus: That's too good to be true!

Reader #6: That reminds me of another one. This babysitter is in a huge house. The kids are asleep in their bedrooms. The telephone rings. When she answers, she hears a weird laugh. (Reader can provide a scary laugh.) Ten minutes later, the telephone rings again, and she hears another weird laugh. (Another laugh, louder and scarier.) This time she calls the operator and asks her to trace the call. Once again, he calls and laughs hysterically. (Laugh again like a homicidal maniac.) The operator interrupts the phone call, yelling to the babysitter, "Get out of that house! The calls are coming from an upstairs private line!"

Chorus: That's too good to be true!

Reader #7: What's scarier than a graveyard? One night a group of bored teens drives to a graveyard. On a dare, one guy tells his girlfriend to stick a knife in the grave. She stabs the knife in the grave and tries to run away. She can't move. Some corpse must be pulling her into the grave! She dies of a heart attack—from fright. Later, the police said that she plunged the knife into her long coat and that prevented her from running away.

Chorus: That's too good to be true!

Additional Urban Legends

For Younger Readers (Ages 6–8)

Urban legends may not be appropriate for younger members. Furthermore, their reading skills will not be advanced enough to perform Reader's Theater. Here are some other suggestions:

Read-aloud. Younger book clubbers will appreciate books by Lee Bennett Hopkins, Joanne Rocklin, and Alvin Schwartz.

Creative dramatics. After telling or reading a story, have the children act out the story.

Arts and crafts. Have the children make stick or paper bag puppets to act out the story.

Recipe. Make a "scary" pot of spaghetti (brains), grapes (eyes), raisins, and other squishy ingredients. Blindfold the students and have them place their hands in the pot for a scary surprise.

Preteen and Teens

Reader's Theater is usually successful for these age groups. No one has to memorize lines or wear costumes. Instead, the group sits in their seats and reads their assigned parts aloud.

The play's the thing. Find a play that appropriate for your readers. Consider writing a short play, or have the group write the play.

Pay for your play. If you have the budget, consider purchasing books that contain RT scripts. Barchers, Black, Bocaz-Larson, Freeman, and Shepherd write helpful books that provide tips and scripts for a wide range of readers.

Prepare the scripts. Make copies of the play for all the members, titling the character's name on the script and underlining her lines.

Rehearse the play.

+ Begin by giving each participant a copy of the play.

+ Read the play aloud to the group, thoroughly and slowly, explaining any unfamiliar words and providing suggestions of readings.

+ Ask for any volunteers for any of the roles. If many want the same roles, produce a fair way to assign parts, such as asking the volunteers to place their names on a paper and having the sponsor draw a name for each part.

+ Maybe you would like to photograph or videotape the program. Make certain that the equipment is working properly, and have replacement batteries available.

The play begins.

+ If possible, arrange the chairs in a circle so that the readers can relate to the other characters.

+ The "clapper" begins the play with the word "Action." The script is read from beginning to end, with no interruptions.

+ The sponsor ends the reading by saying, "Cut! Print!"

Keyword search. Try "reader's theater" as a start, and then try the various other spellings to receive more information.

Works Cited on "Reader's Theater and Urban Legends"

Barchers, Suzanne I. *Scary Readers Theatre*. Santa Barbara, CA: Libraries Unlimited, 1994. Print.
> Thirty scary, multinational urban legends for elementary and middle schools.

Black, Ann N. *Readers Theatre for Middle School Boys: Investigating the Strange and the Mysterious*. Westport, CT: Libraries Unlimited, 2008. Print.
> The author selects classics and provides short author backgrounds and production notes. Also try *More Reader's Theatre for Middle School Boys* (2009).

Bocaz-Larson, D. M. *Freedrama.com*. Web. 22 July 2009.
> Highly recommended Web site that offers free plays for children and teens. The author requests that sponsors ask for written permission by e-mail.

Bocaz-Larson, D. M. *Royalty Free Plays from Freedrama.com*. New York: CreateSpace, 2009. Print.
> These highly recommended scripts do not require written permission from the author.

Brunvand, Jan Harold. *Be Afraid, Be Very Afraid: The Book of Scary Urban Legends*. New York: Norton, 2004. Print.
> The author is an authority on American urban legends. All his books are recommended, including *Encyclopedia of Urban Legends* (2002) and *The Choking Doberman* (2003). The RT script *Too Good to Be True* adapts some of these urban legends.

Fleming, Robert Loren, and Robert F. Boyd Jr. *The Big Book of Urban Legends*. New York: Paradox, 1994. Print.
> Highly readable comic book of urban legends adapted from the works of Jan Harold Brunvand. The RT script *Too Good to Be True* adapts some of these tales.

Freeman, Judy. *Once upon a Time: Using Storytelling, Creative Drama, and Reader's Theater with Children PreK-6*. Westport, CT: Libraries Unlimited, 2007. Print.
> Highly recommended for sponsors whose group includes younger children, providing suggestions for RT, creative dramatics, and storytelling.

Hopkins, Lee Bennett. *Halloween Howls: Holiday Poetry*. I Can Read Book. New York: HarperCollins, 2006. Print.
> Young readers will enjoy these Halloween poems.

Rocklin, Joanne, and JoAnn Adinolfi, ill. *This Book Is Haunted*. I Can Read Book, Level 2. New York: HarperCollins, 2003. Print.
> Young readers can read these violence-free ghost stories.

Schwartz, Alvin. *Ghosts! Ghostly Tales from Folklore*. I Can Read Book, Level 2. New York: HarperCollins, 1993. Print.
> Beginning readers enjoy this one. Older readers will enjoy this series: *Scary Stories to Tell in the Dark* (1981), *More Scary Stories to Tell the in the Dark* (1984), and *Scary Stories 3* (1991).

Shepherd, Aaron. *Readers on Stage*. Friday Harbor, WA: Shepherd, 2004. Print.
> The guru of Reader's Theater promoted the educational appeal of RT. Check out his Web site, www.aaronshep.com/rt.

READING GAMES

For Ages 3–10

Participating in a reading game can be especially motivational for younger readers. Awarding prizes is not necessary. Just display completed reading sheets in a well-viewed area, and many children will gladly participate.

These games are also a way for parents or guardians to participate by reading aloud to their children. Some parents may need some guidance on appropriate books to read, so have some reading lists available. But also allow the children to select their books, demonstrating their skills with the Dewey system, genres, and reading.

Reading Web Site

The book *Games for Reading: Playful Ways to Help Your Child Read* offers many games, with instructions and age levels, including printable coloring pages. The author also provides many educational games on her home page, www.peggykaye.com.

Literature Bingo

- ✦ The object of this reading game is to introduce young readers to literature genres.
- ✦ All blocks must be completed, for a total of 25 books.
- ✦ An adult may read aloud, or a beginning reader can attempt to read at her own level. Each completed square is either signed, stamped, or "stickered."
- ✦ Children will acquire hands-on experience in choosing books.
- ✦ Booktalk various genres so that children can locate age-appropriate authors and titles.
- ✦ If genres don't match your book collection, personalize a Bingo card online ("Literature Bingo Cards")

Safari Reading Game

This reproducible game is designed to keep children reading consistently, regardless of genre or reading level. Readers' ability to choose the reading material is a major advantage of this game.

- ✦ The purpose of the game is to complete all 29 blocks by reading any genre or reading level.
- ✦ The sponsor selects the appropriate reading time. Some younger children need only 10 minutes; others need 30 to 60 minutes.
- ✦ Younger children do not have to read books; instead, an adult may read aloud for the required minutes.
- ✦ When the game is completed, each participant returns the sheet to the sponsor.
- ✦ Sponsor displays all completed pages.

Keyword search. For other online reading games, try searching "reading games for kids."

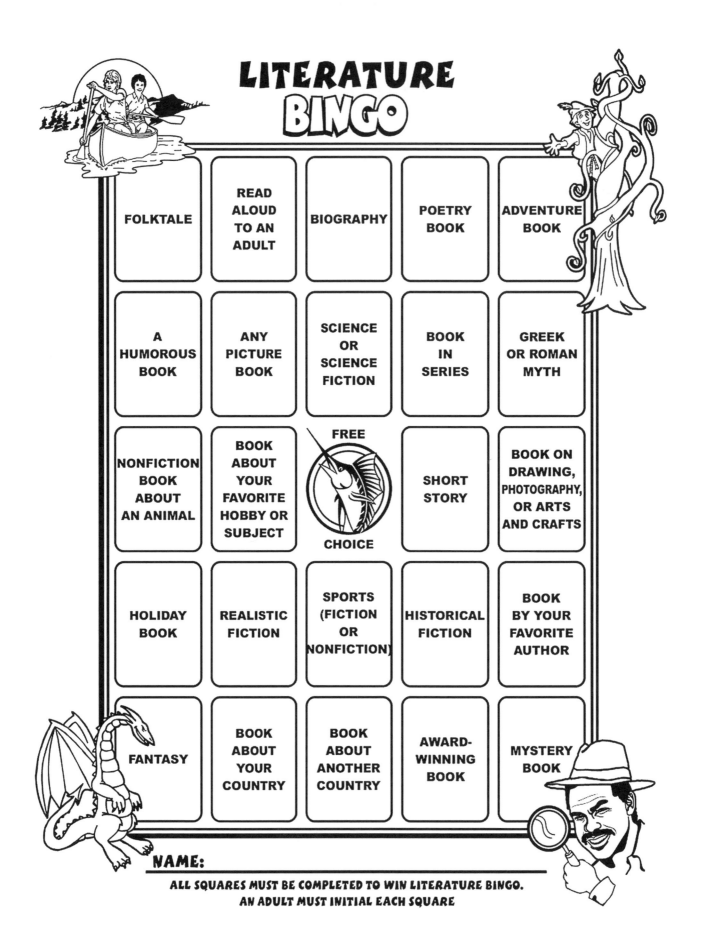

LITERATURE BINGO

FOLKTALE	READ ALOUD TO AN ADULT	BIOGRAPHY	POETRY BOOK	ADVENTURE BOOK
A HUMOROUS BOOK	ANY PICTURE BOOK	SCIENCE OR SCIENCE FICTION	BOOK IN SERIES	GREEK OR ROMAN MYTH
NONFICTION BOOK ABOUT AN ANIMAL	BOOK ABOUT YOUR FAVORITE HOBBY OR SUBJECT	FREE CHOICE	SHORT STORY	BOOK ON DRAWING, PHOTOGRAPHY, OR ARTS AND CRAFTS
HOLIDAY BOOK	REALISTIC FICTION	SPORTS (FICTION OR NONFICTION)	HISTORICAL FICTION	BOOK BY YOUR FAVORITE AUTHOR
FANTASY	BOOK ABOUT YOUR COUNTRY	BOOK ABOUT ANOTHER COUNTRY	AWARD-WINNING BOOK	MYSTERY BOOK

NAME: _____

ALL SQUARES MUST BE COMPLETED TO WIN LITERATURE BINGO.
AN ADULT MUST INITIAL EACH SQUARE

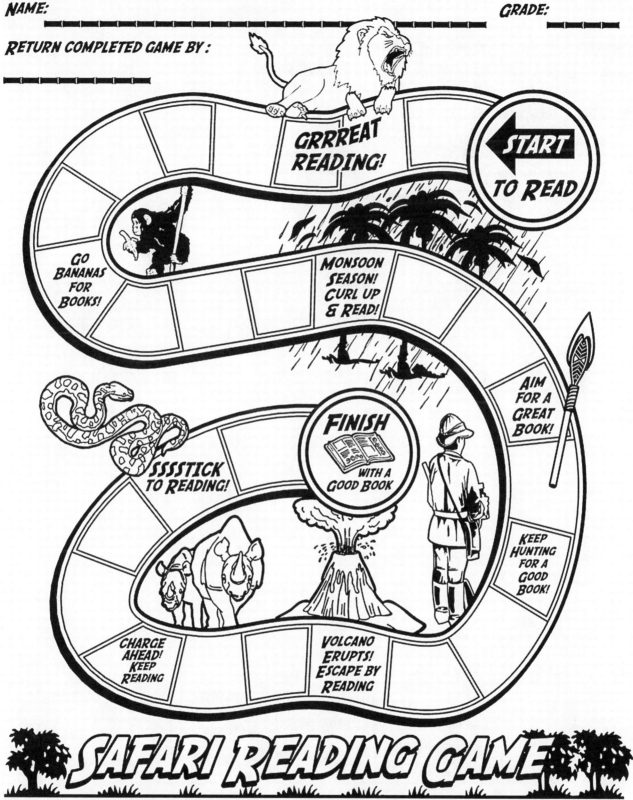

NAME: ▬▬▬▬▬▬▬▬▬▬▬▬▬▬▬▬▬▬▬▬▬▬▬▬▬▬▬▬ GRADE: ▬▬▬▬▬▬

RETURN COMPLETED GAME BY :

▬▬▬▬▬▬▬▬▬▬▬

START TO READ

GRRREAT READING!

GO BANANAS FOR BOOKS!

MONSOON SEASON! CURL UP & READ!

AIM FOR A GREAT BOOK!

SSSSTICK TO READING!

FINISH WITH A GOOD BOOK

KEEP HUNTING FOR A GOOD BOOK!

CHARGE AHEAD! KEEP READING

VOLCANO ERUPTS! ESCAPE BY READING

SAFARI READING GAME

EACH BLOCK REPRESENTS____ MINUTES OF RECREATIONAL READING.
YOU MAY READ ALONE OR HAVE SOMEONE READ TO YOU.
ABOVE ALL, HAVE FUN HUNTING FOR GREAT BOOKS!
An adult must initial each block of time.

Works Cited on "Reading Games"

Kaye, Peggy. *Games for Reading: Playful Ways to Help Your Child Read.* New York: Pantheon, 1984. Print.
> Describes many reading games for all ages.

Kaye, Peggy. Home page. Web. 15 June 2010.
> Offers many free downloadable games, along with instructions and age levels.

"Literature Bingo Cards." *Bingo Card Creator.* Web. 17 May 2010.
> Printable bingo cards for more than 35 activities.

Littlejohn, Carol. "Literature Bingo." Home page. Web. 17 May 2010.
> Game is available online.

Littlejohn, Carol. "Safari Reading Game." Home page. Web. 17 May 2010.
> Game is available online.

SCRAPBOOKING

For All Readers

ScrapBooking (as opposed to scrapbooking) is the process of selecting a book and describing it graphically and textually. This activity encourages creativity and inspires others to read the book. In many ways, ScrapBooking is similar to booktalking because a ScrapBook never reveals the ending of the book. These ScrapBooks can be kept and displayed year after year during special events, but be certain to obtain written permission from students.

History of scrapbooking. In the past, people collected their memories, including recipes, letters, poems, and photographs, in albums or scrapbooks. Marielen Christensen of Spanish Fork, Utah, is credited with being the person who revived interest in scrapbooking. She and her husband opened a scrapbook store in 1981 that is still open today. Today there are many "scrappers" who unite during conventions, retreats, and online ("Scrapbooking").

Materials

These materials are inexpensive and easy to find:

+ Rulers
+ Scissors (straight-edge and decorative-edge)
+ Acid-free glue, adhesive dots, or photo-mounting tape
+ Pencil
+ Eraser
+ Pens in multiple colors
+ Acid-free paper, card stock, and decorative papers in all colors and designs. The album covers can be made from these papers.
+ Hole punchers
+ Ribbon or yarn to tie the album together
+ Cutting map
+ If available, stickers, rub-ons, templates, stamps, brads, lace, wire, fabric

If possible, laminate each page before binding with ribbon.

ScrapBooking

Like booktalking, ScrapBooking is an innovative way to promote books. Here are some suggestions for creative ScrapBooking:

+ **Length.** Each ScrapBook should be about six pages.
+ **Author and title.** The title of the book and the author's name should be on the cover.

- ✦ **Journaling.** *Journaling* is the adding of text to the photograph, drawing, or artifact. The text provides information about the plot, characters, or theme without revealing the ending. Either computer text or student-written text is acceptable, but the text must be readable.

- ✦ **Designed by...** On the back cover, the student writes his name, such as "Designed by...."

- ✦ **Date and grade.** The student adds the date and his grade to the back cover.

- ✦ **Permission slip.** Participants must sign a permission form for any public displays.

- ✦ **Books to consult.** Some recommended authors offer comprehensive and creative ideas for scrapbooking (Check; Lewis; Schuh and Stephani).

- ✦ **Useful Web sites.** Various Web sites provide free information on patterns, events, and blogs ("Scrapbook Directory;" "Scrapbooking, Digital Scrapbooking").

Dewey number. The scrapbook section is 771.46.

Keyword search. For current online resources, search "scrapbooking for kids," "scrapbooking ideas for kids," and "digital scrapbooking kids."

Works Cited on "ScrapBooking"

Check, Laura, and Betsy Day, ill. *Almost-Instant Scrapbooks.* Quick Starts for Kids! Charlotte, VT: Williamson, 2003. Print.
    Provides instructions for creating various types of scrapbooks, with information about collecting and preserving materials, weeding and labeling, and designing pages and covers.

Check, Laura, and Betsy Day, ill. *The Kids' Guide to Making Scrapbooks and Photo Albums! How to Collect, Design, Assemble, Decorate.* A Williamson Kids Can! Book. Charlotte, VT: Williamson, 2002. Print.
    How to collect, design, assemble, and decorate scrapbooks.

Lewis, Amanda, and Esperanca Melo, ill. *Making Memory Books.* Kids Can Do It. Buffalo, NY: Kids Can, 1999. Print.
    Teaches how to create different types of memory books, including little gift books, accordion-fold books, and memory albums.

Schuh, Debby, and Julie Stephani. *Kids Scrapbooking Easy as 1–2-3.* Iola, WI: Krause, 2002. Print.
    Provides instructions, ideas, and patterns, including glossary and resources.

"Scrapbooking." *Wikipedia.* Web. 18 May 2010.
    History of scrapbooking, with some recommended Web sites.

"Scrapbooking, Digital Scrapbooking." *Smilebox.* Web. 26 Sept. 2009.
    Easy, creative scrapbooking, with patterns.

"Scrapbooking Directory." *Scrapbooking-directory.com.* Web. 26 Sept. 2009.
    Provides information on digital scrapbooking, events, magazines, contests, and blogs.

SOAP OPERA

For Preteens and Teens

The soap opera is an excellent device for creative writing and performing. This activity will take at least four to six meetings. The goal is for the group to write, edit, produce, and tape a 15-minute show. The sponsor has the responsibility to guide the group throughout the process. All participants use their writing, performing, and reading skills (Curtis 1–3).

History. A *soap opera* is an ongoing work of dramatic fiction with a high concentration on drama. In many ways, a soap opera is similar to a book series. The name "soap opera" comes from American radio soap advertisements aired during these dramas. To many, a soap opera is a derogatory term, but these stories are performed throughout the globe, in all languages and formats. The Latin American version of soap opera—called a *telenovela*—is one of the most-watched genres of television ("Soap Opera").

Plots. The plots usually involve a romance and a rivalry. Many plots contain a car accident or murder, but these developments usually take place offstage, with the dialogue providing an explanation. Most soap operas end with a climatic cliffhanger ("Soap Opera").

Restrictions. The sponsor must limit some of the characteristics of most soap operas. For example, your soap opera will not be ongoing unless the group decides to continue the story. Also, many soap operas deal with sexual topics that will not be appropriate.

Examples

These examples may provide you with the direction you need to plan your soap opera. Perhaps you can call the soap opera "*School Daze*" and select one of these plots:

✦ What happens when the most popular group in school turns out to be vampires or zombies? (This activity could involve elaborate makeup.)

✦ What happens when a boy or girl enrolls in the school and becomes the reason for a feud between two rivals?

✦ Why does Parker (boy or girl) act so strangely? Could it be that Parker has an evil twin?

✦ What if Little Red Riding Hood goes to school and meets a handsome Wolf?

✦ What if a literary character (Harry Potter?) or an historical figure came to your school? What would he think, and whom would he meet?

Preproduction

✦ **The Story.** First, guide the students into agreeing on a plot, location, and list of characters. The characters interact by chance meetings at family or school gatherings. The sponsor writes down suggestions and, after all the ideas are discussed, is responsible for approving the final script.

- **Four acts.** Divide the plot into four acts, with a beginning and a cliffhanging ending in each act. Divide the students into four groups to write each act; perhaps each group will assign one writer to complete the act. All the dialogue and stage directions must be written. Cue cards may be written later for the actors if they have difficulty learning their lines.

- **Prepare the final script.** After each group presents each of the four acts, the sponsor reads the script aloud to the group. Correct any weaknesses, and link all the characters into a coherent script.

- **Casting the parts.** Ask for volunteers as actors. If two or more want the same part or character, hold a quick audition, assign the part, and assure the others that there will receive sufficient roles for everyone. Just make certain that everyone contributes, since there are many useful jobs: assistant director, film crew, cue card technician, sound effects director, music director, end-of-credits sponsor, costume designer, and set designer. Many students can do two assignments.

Production

The filming begins. This activity should be loose and fun. Don't worry about mistakes. The most important activity is the creative writing, not the performing. If you do not have access to filming equipment, you can either audiotape the soap opera or present it as Reader's Theater. After acquiring written permission, librarians can catalog these films or tapes into the library.

Works Cited for "Soap Opera"

Curtis, Jerry. *50 Ways to Stimulate Low-Ability and Reluctant Learners: A Resource Book for Secondary School Teachers.* Unionville, NY: Trillium, 1989. Print.

> Highly recommended for inspiring reading activities, including writing a soap opera. (Amazon lists the author as "Cris," but title page lists author as "Jerry Curtis." Locate the book using the title.)

"Soap Opera." *Wikipedia*. Web. 17 May 2010.

> Describes the history and types of soap operas.

STORYTELLING

For All Ages

Storytelling is a useful art and activity that is successful for all ages. All children and young adults can develop their listening skills in oral literature and learn narration techniques (such as repetition).

History. Storytelling is a universal tradition. It probably began with prehistoric humans who sought to communicate their experiences. Anyone can tell a story, but storytelling is an art that demands discipline and wisdom. Perhaps the most recognized authority on storytelling is Marie Shedlock, with her 1915 book, *The Art of the Storyteller.*

During the past century, many librarians (Anne Carroll Moore, Elin Greene, and Augusta Baker) also recognized the importance of storytelling as part of the library storytime experience. They established many of the practices that are still followed today, from memorizing a favorite story to restraining the emotions when telling the story.

However, most educators and storytellers agree that there are many different ways to tell a story and that no particular way is the right way.

Telling a Tale

✦ **Finding stories.** To find a folktale, search under Dewey number 398.2. For short stories, try 823 or 811. Check the library, using the keywords "short stories" and "folk tales." Pick a story that you can tell again and again, perhaps something from your culture.

✦ **Practice makes perfect.** Practice the selected story again and again. You don't have to memorize it, but you do need to know the story intimately.

Follow these storytelling suggestions for great results (Ellis "How"):

✦ **First impression.** Try to capture the audience's interest immediately. Perhaps you can tell how you discovered this story or supply the background of the author. You can start off with a question and ask for input or for the audience to suggest answers. A relevant poem or riddle might provide the beginning. Whatever you decide to say, you need to plan your beginning so that you can make a smooth transition to your story.

✦ **Use your presence.** Use all your tools: your body, your voice, your expressions, and especially your imagination.

✦ **Audience involvement.** Involve the audience. Make direct eye contact. Have audience members become a character, repeat a phrase, stand up, or clap their hands.

✦ **End with a bang.** End your story with a quick finish: "And that's why…"; "To this day…"; or "People still say…." Give a pause and then bow to the audience. Wait for the applause!

Audience Participation Stories

Many stories involve audience participation. These participation stories require children to develop their listening skills, and some acting skills may also come to play. Whatever happens, it's all fun.

- ✦ **Say it again.** One of the main features of a folktale is its repetition (e.g., "Trip trap trip trap trip trap" in the Norwegian folktale "The Three Billy Goats Gruff"). Encourage audience members to join in by motioning with your hands that they should join in.

- ✦ **Use cumulative stories.** Cumulative folktales are perfect for audience participation. For example, the story "The House That Jack Built" adds more characters as the story continues (the farmer, the wife, the daughter, the farmhand, the rooster, the dog, the cat, the mouse, a piece of cheese). The characters can be puppets, flannel board pieces, or even the children. Have each child stand when his part is read, finally sitting on reaching the last phrase, "This is the house that Jack built." More and more characters join in, and the fun begins. Other cumulative folktales are "The Great Enormous Turnip" and "Too Much Noise."

- ✦ **Songs.** For participatory songs, try "I Know an Old Lady" and "Old MacDonald Had a Farm." If puppets or props are not available, the audience can creatively dramatize the story.

- ✦ **Recommended online resources.** Two Web sites, Story-Lovers (www.story-lovers.com/index/html) and LibrarySpot (www.libraryspot.com/features/storytellingfeature.htm), offer a variety of tips and stories ("Fairy Tales;" "Storytelling"). Another useful resource is *Joining In!* (Miller), a compilation of audience participation stories told by renowned storytellers.

- ✦ **Attend storytelling festivals.** Stories must be seen and heard. Check out your local area for the best storytellers, and see their performances. Consider attending the annual National Storytelling Festival in Jonesborough, Tennessee, during the first weekend in October. This festival in considered one of the best.

- ✦ **Sponsor a storytelling festival.** Teach the group the basics of storytelling: encourage group members to select a story and to tell that story to the group. If all goes well, consider adding another performance, this time with an audience. Record and photograph the festival for a permanent record.

Keyword search. For current online information, search "storytelling," "storytelling for kids," and "audience participation stories."

Works Cited on "Storytelling"

"About the Festival." *National Storytelling Festival—Jonesborough, TN.* Web. 26 Sept. 2009.
Renowned storytellers tell their favorite tales during the first weekend in October.

Adams, Pam. *This Is the House That Jack Built.* Classic Books with Holes. Swindon, United Kingdom: Child's Play, 2007. Print.
One of many versions of this cumulative tale.

Adams, Pam. *Old MacDonald Had a Farm.* Classic Books with Holes. Swindon, United Kingdom: Child's Play, 2007. Print.
A favorite nursery song that encourages audience participation.

Adams, Pam. *There Was an Old Lady.* Classic Books with Holes. Swindon, United Kingdom: Child's Play, 2007. Print.
Another cumulative song you can use.

Ellis, Brian "Fox." "How to Tell a Tale: Storytelling Basics." Home page. Web. 21 Sept. 2009.
A storyteller gives many helpful hints on how to tell a story.

Ellis, Brian "Fox." *Learning from the Land: Teaching Ecology through Stories and Activities.* Santa Barbara, CA: Teacher Ideas, 1998. Print.
This book includes the cumulative story "The Enormous Turnip."

"Fairy Tales, Folklore, Fables, Nursery Rhymes, Myths, Legends, Bible and Classics." *Story Lovers World: Connecting People Through Stories.* Web. 28 Jan. 2011.
This Web site is a valuable tool for resources on storytelling.

McGovern, Ann, and Simon Taback, ill. *Too Much Noise.* New York: Sandpiper, 1992. Print.
Children can participate in various noises, including the teakettle whistling and the door squeaking.

Miller, Teresa, with assistance from Anne Pellowski; Norma Live, ed. *Joining In: An Anthology of Audience Participation Stories and How to Tell Them.* Cambridge, MA: Yellow Moon, 1988. Print.
Group-participation stories by renowned storytellers Heather Forest, Linda Goss, Laura Simms, and Doug Lipman.

Shedlock, Marie. *The Art of the Story-Teller. Digital Library.* Web. 21 Sept. 2009.
This Irish storyteller wrote a book in 1915 that still remains one of the classics about storytelling.

"Storytelling: How to Tell a Tale." *LibrarySpot.* Web. 18 May 2010.
Helpful tips and story recommendations.

TALENT SHOW

For All Ages

Initiating a talent show is a way to awaken students' interests and hobbies. Students can demonstrate their special talents at the beginning of each meeting, during a designated day, or during a school assembly.

Talent Show Ideas

Many young people will say they do not have a talent. Maybe they think their skills are of no interest to their peers. A talent show or demonstration can change that. Some talent show ideas are offered on the PackNight Web site ("Talent Show Ideas"):

- Magic tricks
- Comedy
- Performing in skits or plays
- Demonstrating American Sign Language
- Collecting baseball cards or any tangible objects
- Playing an instrument
- Painting or drawing
- Photography
- Writing and reading stories
- Demonstrating quilting or sewing
- Cooking
- Creating wood crafts
- Speaking another language
- Storytelling
- Puppet show
- Dancing
- Singing
- Arts and crafts

Keyword search. Use "talent show ideas" and "talent show ideas kids" for an online search. Books and Web sites are available on specific talents, such as "magic" or "photography."

Works Cited for "Talent Show"

"Talent Show Ideas." *PackNight*. Web. 22 July 2009.
    Multiple ideas for talent shows, including stories, skits, puppets, magic tricks, and music.

TRIAL BY JURY

For All Readers

This activity is similar to the mystery activity game, but it is more informal and easier to prepare and conduct. The group becomes members of a jury, listening to both sides of a case. The sponsor is the judge (Curtis 17). After the trial, the jury deliberates in order to decide whether the accused is innocent or guilty. In some court cases, the verdict must be unanimous; in other courts, the majority can decide the verdict. A supermajority is a two-thirds majority. A hung jury occurs when the jurors can't agree on a decision.

Preproduction

+ **Length.** This activity can last for several meetings or, for younger readers, one meeting.

+ **Select a suitable crime.** Save the more graphic crimes for the teens. Instead, younger readers can solve crimes that involve theft. For this reason, this section is divided into younger and older readers with suggested resources.

+ **Let the age fit the crime.** Most crimes will not appeal to all ages. However, some true-life mysteries can be used successfully. In 1872, the crew of the ship *Mary Celeste* mysteriously disappeared, although the ship is found undamaged and carrying uneaten food. Younger readers can use the picture book *The Mary Celeste: An Unsolved Mystery from History,* which cites six different theories that might explain the abandoned ship (Yolen). Older readers can do further research on the mystery, split into teams, and debate the theories, concluding with a vote on the reasonable outcome. Tweak the reading activity to fit the age of your group, using the trial for only one meeting or several.

+ **Select suitable lawyers.** If lawyers are required, the sponsor must choose as wisely as any judge. Choose people who are articulate and who can analyze from different perspectives. You can even choose a team of lawyers. The jury consists of all types of learners.

+ **The verdict is...** In advance, the sponsor determines whether the verdict is unanimous, a majority or a supermajority, depending on the size and age of the group.

For Younger Readers (Ages 6–8)

At this age, children know little about crime. Use these suggestions to keep this activity fun and educational.

+ **Keep it simple.** Keep the story simple, with many illustrations.

+ **Keep it simple, twice.** Don't assign lawyers or a jury. This concept may be too confusing.

+ **Critical thinking.** This group probably won't be able to reach a unanimous decision. However, ask the children who volunteer to explain their answers. This activity is designed to teach critical-thinking skills.

Preteens

This group will be able to understand the concepts of a trial and of a jury system. Provide them some background on the criminal system by looking up "jury" in a general encyclopedia. Share with them specific information and answer pertinent questions.

+ **Make it simple.** The lawyers may not need to be selected for this age group. The sponsor can present both sides and have the group vote guilty or for acquittal.

+ **Perry Mason gets his trial.** If lawyers are selected, it might be beneficial for the group to watch a show that demonstrates lawyers presenting evidence. The old standby is *Perry Mason*, the longest-running American TV series about a lawyer. The episodes are brief and are in black and white.

+ **You be the jury.** A series of books, *You Be the Jury*, is written just for this age group (Miller).

+ **Folktale puzzles.** Shannon has written a series of books that provides folktale puzzles from around the world: *Stories to Solve* (2000), *More Stories to Solve* (2001), *True Lies* (1998), and *More True Lies* (2008).

+ **Justice riddles.** Check out *The Cow of No Color*, an intriguing book that presents international riddles and justice tales (Jaffe and Zeitlin).

+ **Virtual trials.** Select a historical or fictional character, and put that person on trial. It would be particularly relevant if the group were studying this person in school. For example, is Adolph Hitler guilty of genocide? Is the mythical figure Hercules a murderer, or is he responsible for saving humanity? Is Paris responsible for beginning the Trojan War? The defense and prosecuting attorneys must present evidence to persuade the jury.

Teens

This age group can handle more complicated trials on difficult issues. For this reason, the trial may last for several meetings.

+ *Be the Jury*. Consider using the *Be the Judge/Be the Jury* series, particularly the book *The Sacco-Vanzetti Trial* (Rappaport). Each book in the series provides exact trial testimony and explains the complete judicial system, including the inquest and the actual trial.

+ *The Jury Box*. *The Jury Box* is a party game that can be used with young adults. The players are the jury, so this game doesn't require lawyers. Each box comes with six different court cases, an outline of the state's evidence against the defendant, along with two pictures of the crime scene. Ballots are provided for the jury to vote guilty or not guilty (Post).

+ **Real-life crimes.** These trials can be complex and detailed, with lawyers presenting photographs and charts. For example, did Lee Harvey Oswald kill President John Kennedy? Or you can present a controversial issue and have the lawyers take different viewpoints. Should the government fund stem cell research? Should a ban on smoking in public places be enforced? What about a trial on the pros and cons of capital punishment?

Keyword search. For an online update, try "jury by trial for young people."

Works Cited for "Jury by Trial"

Curtis, Jerry. *50 Ways to Stimulate Low-Ability and Reluctant Learners: A Resource Book for Secondary School Teachers.*
Unionville, NY: Trillium, 1989. Print.
Author's brief reading activity provides the suggestion of "jury by trial."

Jaffe, Nina, and Steve Zeitlin. *The Cow of No Color.* New York: Puffin, 2007. Print.
Preteens can discuss riddles and justice tales from around the world.

Miller, Marvin. *You Be the Jury.* New York: Scholastic, 1992. Print.
Series designed for preteens.

Perry Mason. Fancast. Web. 20 May 2010.
Watch *Perry Mason* TV episodes online.

Post, Roy. *The Jury Box.* Web. 21 Aug. 2009.
For a cost, this site provides online party game for teens.

Rappaport, Doreen. *The Sacco-Vanzetti Trial.* Be the Judge/Be the Jury. New York: HarperCollins, 1992. Print.
This series for preteens and teens provides testimony, photographs, prints, diagrams, and newspaper articles.

Shannon, George. *Stories to Solve.* New York: Greenwillow, 2000. Print.
Other recommended books include *More Stories to Solve* (2001); *True Lies: 18 Tales for You to Judge* (1998); and *More True Lies: 18 Tales for You to Judge* (2008). Series designed for preteens.

Watt, Jim. *The Mary Celeste: Fact, Not Fiction.* Web. 13 June 2010.
Provides the "true" story of the *Mary Celeste,* with information about Captain Briggs. Older readers can conduct a trial based on Captain Brigg's responsibility for the nautical disaster.

Yolen, Jane, and Heidi Elisabeth Yolen Stemple, ill. *The Mary Celeste: An Unsolved Mystery from History.* New York: Simon & Schuster, 1999. Print.
Younger readers will enjoy trying to solve this true-life mystery. Also useful for any age exploring the mystery genre.

YOUNG AUTHORS AND ILLUSTRATORS

For All Ages

Many young authors and illustrators join book clubs. Most are looking for an outlet for their creativity. Why not celebrate these artists and their talents? The best way to become a better writer (poet, illustrator) is to practice, practice, practice. If these students are discouraged, they won't continue perfecting their craft. Try some of these activities, even if some members choose not to participate.

Guidelines for Writing and Illustrating

If you need specific guidelines for all writing and illustrating activities, consider these rules ("Writing Contests"):

✦ Manuscripts or drawings must be the author's own work. A participant can request that an adult proofread her work, but the work must represent the author's ability. Each author must sign a statement that the work is solely his work. If the work is accepted, the author must grant written permission to print the work in either a journal or bound book.

✦ Eligible participants must meet a certain age requirement.

✦ Participants must refrain from profanity, slander, or graphic violence. The editor has the right to edit the entry.

✦ The format must be clearly defined (e.g., manuscripts must be no longer than 1,500 words). Will nonfiction entries be accepted? If so, state that the text must be factually accurate and that credit must be given to any sources used by the writer.

✦ Comic books, graphic novels, poetry, stories, and books (fiction or nonfiction) are included and encouraged.

Comics or Graphic Novels

A *comic* is a graphic medium in which cartoon images are presented in a sequential narration. A *graphic novel* is a long comic book, usually bound, telling one story. Graphic novels are now being used in the classroom as a way to encourage reading, especially for students struggling with language acquisition. Although some graphic novels are violent in content, many are free of violence and suitable for all ages.

✦ **Recommended Web sites.** Some helpful Web sites teach drawing and narration and provide a list of recommended resources (Crawford and Weiner; Gardner).

✦ **Internet resource guide.** One college student created an online resource for teachers, offering details on graphic novel genres, including how to create comics (Lavin).

✦ **Teaching guide.** Want a step-by-step teaching guide to teaching the graphic novel? Try downloading Scholastic's teaching guide, using the *Bone* series by Jeff Smith at www. scholastic.com/bone (Crawford and Weiner).

Web Publishing

What about Web publishing? Young people can submit their drawings, stories, and poems to the sponsor. Perhaps the group members can type their own stories as part of the project. The sponsor can put these materials on a local Web site.

✦ **Guidelines.** Never use students' last names or personal information. Never publish personal Web sites for students. Most of all, written permission from an adult parent or guardian must be obtained before a student's work is published on the Web (Peyton).

✦ **Online student publishing.** Offers a free 12- or 16-page storybook at www.studentpub lishing.com designed by young writers. Extra copies are printed for a fee ("Free Student Publishing").

Writing Activities

Do these activities as a group activity, or encourage individuals to submit their work.

✦ **Happily ever after.** For younger writers (ages 5–9), consider using the book *Once upon a Time: Writing Your Own Fairy Tale* (Lowen). Read the book aloud to participants, spending time on the techniques of writing an original fairy tale (setting, characters, plot, dialogue, warnings, magic, greed, tricks, secret, repetition, mistakes, and problem solving with a satisfying finale). Publish the original fairy tales (with illustrations) in one booklet.

✦ **Edit a booklet.** Become an editor of a booklet of short entries of poetry, illustrations, and short stories. If possible, bind the entry at a local printing store and add the entry to the library. Guidelines might be distributed in advance so that the artists will know the boundaries.

✦ **Interactive poetry.** Encourage the group to write poetry. Explain that poems don't always rhyme and that each line represents a thought or idea. Create an interactive poetry project to encourage children (ages 7–12) to write poetry by using the "Origami Poetry Writer." Students create an "origami poetry writer" from a sheet of paper, writing one word on each flap and using those words in the poem (Mancini-Wilson 73–77).

Publishing Permission Form. A sample Publishing Permission Form is presented at the back of the book. Obtain a signed permission slip before displaying or using any project.

Keyword search

✦ For current Web sites on comics and graphic novels, search "web design comic," "lesson plans comic books," and "lesson plans graphic novels."

✦ For Web publishing, search "student Web publishing."

✦ For writing contests, search "writing contests," "writing contests for kids," and "writing contests for teens." For contests that offer money and have deadlines, add the current year to the search.

✦ For contests, search "contests for kids" and "contests for teens." For contests that offer money and have deadlines, add the current year to the search.

Works Cited for "Young Authors and Illustrators"

Crawford, Phillip, and Stephen Weiner. "Using the Graphic Novel in the Classroom." *Graphix*. Web. 24 Dec. 2009.
Download this free PDF file from Jeff Smith's Web site.

"Free Student Publishing." *Studentpublishing*. Web. 24 Dec. 2009.
Offers a free 12 or 16 page storybook at www.studentpublishing.com.

Gardner, Traci. "Book Report Alternative: Comic Strips and Cartoon Squares." *ReadWriteThink*. Web. 24 Dec. 2004.
Two 50-minute sessions on creating comic strips that feature characters in books.

Lavin, Mike. "Graphic Novels: Resources for Teachers and Librarians." *State University of New York at Buffalo*. Web. 24 Dec. 2009.
Highly recommended Web site that provides multiple Internet resources on graphic novels, including "How to Create Comics."

Lowen, Nancy. *Once upon a Time: Writing Your Own Fairy Tale*. Writer's Toolbox. Mankato, MN: Picture Window, 2009. Print.
Picture book explores tools that beginning writers need. Four writing exercises are included.

Mancini-Wilson, Debbie. *Color My World: An Interactive Poetry Book for Kids of All Ages*. Pittsburgh, PA: Harmony, 2007. Print.
This spiral-bound book offers many fun activities for writing poetry, especially the "origami poetry writer."

Payton, Tammy. "Empowering Student Learning with Web Publishing." *Loogootee West*. Web. 24 Dec. 2009.
Provides guidelines for Web publishing, including a "Students Permission Form."

CHAPTER 6

Cover to Cover: Recommended Group-Reads

For Preteens and Teens

These recommended group-reads have been given careful consideration. All books are listed alphabetically by the author's last name, followed by recommended ages, booktalk, and a note with suggestions for the group-read.

One of the criteria for a group-read is that the book must stimulate thought-provoking questions and high-level discussions. Using paperback books cuts the expenses of a group-read.

Anderson, Laurie Halse. *Chains: Seeds of America*. **New York: Simon & Schuster, 2008. Ages 12+.**

Historical fiction.

Booktalk: If the American Revolution is sparked by freedom, why can't slaves be part of that liberty? Isabelle and her disabled sister, Ruth, are the property of cruel owners who are secretly spying for the British. Another slave, named Curzon, tries to persuade Isabelle to spy for the patriots. All Isabelle wants is freedom for herself and Ruth. Eventually, Isabelle pays a terrible price for choosing sides. How can Isabelle destroy these chains?

Note: This book begins in New York City in May 1776 and ends in January 1777. Isabelle is a fictional character, but her horrific story of beatings and torture by her masters are based on historical accounts. Although Isabelle is scarred on her cheek with the letter "I" for "Insolence," she manages to remain brave and strong. Her story continues with *Forge* (2009). There is a helpful appendix with frank facts about the real story of slaves in North America. Visit the author's home page at www.writerlady.com.

Appelt, Kathi, with David Small, ill. *The Underneath*. **New York: Atheneum, 2008. Ages 9–12.**

Fantasy.

Booktalk: A pregnant calico cat has been abandoned by the side of the road. She meets a dog that has been abused. Together, they make a life, teaching kittens not to venture from underneath their house. The owner of the house, Gar Face, cares only about himself and capturing the King Alligator. If Gar Face discovers the kittens, he will use the kittens as alligator bait!

Note: This beautiful southern gothic tale needs to be discussed chapter by chapter. Three separate stories occur but are blended into a satisfying ending. Gar Face owns the abused dog, Ranger, but the reader discovers that Gar Face has also been abused. Like Captain Ahab, Gar Face is obsessed with capturing an alligator—even if he must use animals as bait. In spite of the horrifying abuse presented within the text, love and sacrifice are the main themes.

Collins, Suzanne. *The Hunger Games*. **New York: Scholastic, 2008. Ages 13+.**

Science fiction.

Booktalk: Get ready for the Hunger Games! Sixteen-year-old Katniss volunteers her services after her younger sister Prim is selected. She barely knows the baker's son, Peeta, but he is also selected. Together they will fight to the death. But, the question is, can or will they kill each other? Gladiators, anyone?

Note: In a future North America, the rulers of Panem maintain control through a televised event that pits teens against each other; the fittest will win the tournament. Each chapter ends with a cliffhanger. A book club could be named after the title of this book—as long as you serve snacks! The series continues with *Catching Fire* (2009) and *Mockingjay* (2010). Visit the author's home page at www.suzannecollinsbooks.com and, also, the Web site for "hungry" fans at www.mockingjay.net.

Gaiman, Neil, with Dave McKean, ill. *The Graveyard Book*. New York: HarperCollins, 2008. Ages 9–12.

Mystery; horror.

Booktalk: What's it like to live in a graveyard? Ask Nobody Owens. That's right. Nobody Owens. Everyone calls him Bod. That is, the spirits of the graveyard call him Bod. Bod's parents have been murdered, and the spirits have adopted this live baby. But the murderer, Jack, is on the lookout for Bod. Will Jack find Bod, or will the spirits protect Bod?

Note: This Newbery Award winner is a good selection for boys, and many book clubs use this as a group-read. However, be careful about using this book with sensitive souls who might be frightened by graveyards, death, and spirits. Check out Gaiman's home page at www. MouseCircus.com.

Gratz, Alan. *Samurai Shortstop*. New York: Penguin, 2006. Ages 13+.

Sports; historical fiction.

Booktalk: "The secret to catching a ball/Lies with the willow/Swaying in the wind." Toyo appreciates this haiku while he learns the way of the warrior. He comes from a samurai family that is adjusting to the modern values of Japan. After his uncle's heroic suicide, Toyo is expected to help his father accomplish his suicide. The idea fills Toyo with horror. Can baseball help Toyo become both a man and a warrior?

Note: This debut book is recommended for a father-son group-read because of its theme. Can a father pass on the knowledge of how to be a man? Toyo Shimada, 15, is growing up in Tokyo in the 1890s, when the emperor has outlawed the samurai tradition of his ancestors. The book begins with Toyo's uncle performing *suppuku*, a ritual involving disembowelment and decapitation. Graphic violence continues throughout the book, including brutal hazing inflicted on students of traditional samurai arts. However, all the violence is based on historical evidence, as explained in the notes. This book not only is an engrossing read but also demands discussion, especially between men and boys. Baseball is a favorite pastime for both Japanese and Americans; Toyo learns to apply his samurai arts to baseball and becomes a man.

Gresh, Lois H. *The Twilight Companion: The Unauthorized Guide to the Series*. New York: St. Martin, 2008. Ages 10+.

Horror; nonfiction.

Booktalk: Whether you've read the *Twilight* series by Stephenie Meyer doesn't matter. This book explains vampires, werewolves, zombies, and so many other things you are just dying to know about!

Note: A light-hearted look at horror, monsters, and seances, providing a quick read for reluctant readers and possibly leading to reading the *Twilight* series (and other horror romances).

Hiaasen, Carl. *Scat*. New York: Knopf, 2009. Ages 9–12.

Mystery.

Booktalk: Mrs. Starch is known as the school's meanest (and best) teacher. One day she mysteriously disappears on a field trip. Everyone knows that Duane is responsible. The day before her disappearance, he bit (and swallowed!) a pencil that Mrs. Starch was holding. Is Duane responsible for the mysterious disappearance of his teacher? Nick and Marta believe Duane is innocent. Can they prove it?

Note: The author provides humor within a well-developed mystery that involves ecology, particularly the extinction of the Florida panther. The characters are also well developed, especially Nick, whose father lost an arm during the Iraq war. The title, *Scat*, refers to panther dung as well as to a message to hopeful oil drillers to "Scat!" Useful for all types of groups because of thought-provoking discussions about ecology, extinction, posttraumatic stress, and authoritative teachers who are unlikable but skillful.

Jacques, Brian, and Bret Blevins, ill. *Redwall: The Graphic Novel*. New York: Philomel, 2007. Ages 9+.

Graphic novel; fantasy.

Booktalk: Matthias the mouse wants to become a warrior. He wants to be just like Martin, a legendary mouse from Redwall. But nothing ever happens at the Redwall Abbey. That is, nothing ever happens until the evil rat Cluny appears. Maybe Matthias can become a hero after all.

Note: If a graphic novel is selected, why not choose a classic? The *Redwall* series contains rodent adventures that never stop, making this an exciting read for reluctant readers, but mature readers will enjoy the complex plots. Visit the author's Web site at www.redwall.org for more information.

Lockhart, E. *The Disreputable History of Frankie Landau-Banks*. New York: Hyperion, 2008. Ages 13+.

Realistic fiction.

Booktalk: Everyone thinks Frankie is a pretty girl with no brains. Even her boyfriend thinks she is just a dumb "Bunny Rabbit." Then Frankie discovers the secret society called the Loyal Order of the Basset Hounds. She also discovers that she will never become a member because she is female. So she secretly plots to undo this society. How? That's for Frankie to know and for you to find out!

Note: This book has an unusual plot because it discusses secret societies within prestigious colleges and private schools. The endnote presents the author's sources for her writing about boarding schools, boys, clubs, pranks, and interventionist art. These sources and ideas can lead to intriguing discussions about secret societies. Its lack of profanity and sexual scenes make this recommended reading for a mother-daughter group-read.

Magoon, Kekla. *The Rock and the River*. New York: Aladdin, 2009. Ages 12+.

Historical fiction.

Booktalk: Thirteen-year-old Sam is between a rock and a river. He has two choices. Should he accept his father's peaceful means of demonstrating for civil rights? Or should he accept his brother's way? His brother belongs to the Black Panthers, a group with a more violent agenda. What will Sam choose? What is his path?

Note: This book takes place in Chicago in the 1960s and presents a sympathetic portrayal of both sides of the civil rights struggle. Sam's father is an activist who personally knows Martin Luther King Jr. Sam's brother, 17-year-old Stick, is enthralled with the Black Panther organization, especially after Dr. King's assassination. Many important questions and discussions about this period in American history can evolve from a reading of this book. A helpful author's note follows.

Meminger, Neesha. *Shine, Coconut Moon*. New York: McElderry, 2009. Ages 13+.

Realistic fiction.

Booktalk: Samar—called Sam—has a great life living with her mother and being around her best friend, Molly, and her family. Then 9/11 happens. A week later, a turbaned stranger comes to her door and says he is her Uncle Sandeep. What is going on? Suddenly Sam wants to know about her Indian heritage and the Sikh religion. She just doesn't realize how difficult it is going to be.

Note: Samar Ahluwahlia, an Indian American of Punjabi heritage, has no knowledge of her past because her single mother kept her from her relatives. Eventually she learns about her family's religion and background, discovering that she is a "coconut"—brown on the outside, white on the inside. Regardless of her color, she can still shine like a coconut moon. Recommended especially as a mother-daughter group-read. Contains some profanity, but issues of family conflict, racism, ethnicity, and war will provoke many discussions. (*Sikh* is pronounced "sik.")

Mortenson, Greg, and David Oliver Relin. Adapted by Sarah Thomson. *Three Cups of Tea: One Man's Journey to Change the World...One Child at a Time*. Young Reader's ed. New York: Puffin, 2009. Ages 9–12.

Biography.

Booktalk: In Pakistan and in its neighboring countries, there is a certain ritual or ceremony. With the first cup of tea, you are a stranger. With the second cup, you are a friend. With the third cup, you are family. Greg Mortenson becomes "family" because he keeps returning to Pakistan to build schools. Do you know how he builds schools? Thanks to people like you—who give pennies!

Note: Greg Mortenson began as a mountain climber, climbing the K2 summit to place an amber necklace that had belonged to his deceased sister. Instead, he wandered into a small village in Pakistan and was greeted with a cup of butter tea. He observed a school that had no building, books, or supplies. He vowed to return with money and supplies to build a school. At first, only American school children realized the importance of Greg's mission, donating pennies to the cause. The book emphasizes that a dream can become a reality if everyone (including children) contributes. Contains map, photographs, glossary, character list, and a reader's guide. The sequel is *Stones into Schools: Promoting Peace through Books, not Bombs, in Afghanistan and Pakistan* (2009).

Myers, Walter Dean. *Dope Sick*. **New York: HarperTeen, 2009. Ages 13+.**

Realistic fiction.

Booktalk: Lil J is in big trouble. His friend Rico has killed a cop. Lil J is wounded and dope sick. On the run, Lil J meets a stranger who seems to know everything about his past and future. What if he could change the past? Would that change his future?

Note: Without using profanity or violence, this brief, tight book pulls no punches. Some great discussions could evolve: Who is the stranger? Is he a spirit, an angel, or just an aware person? What choices could Lil J have made that would have prevented this catastrophe? More questions than answers, but that's what makes this a good group-read. Visit the author's home page at www.walterdeanmyers.net.

Myers, Walter Dean, and Javaka Steptoe, ill. *Amiri and Odette: A Love Story*. **New York: Scholastic, 2009. Ages 12+.**

Poetry; romance.

Booktalk: Amiri falls in love with Odette at first sight at the Swan Lake Projects. But Big Red, a crack dealer, thinks he owns Odette. Can their love survive?

Note: A perfect picture book of hip-hop poetry (with a dash of Shakespeare) presented with raw, gritty images that appear to dance on the pages. Discussions on the Russian composer Tchaikovsky, *Swan Lake, West Side Story, Romeo and Juliet,* and the Russian folktale of Odette ("the good swan") can thrive. Steptoe's illustrations use acrylic paint on slabs of asphalt with urban collages of candy wrappers, newspaper, plastic bags, and jewelry. So many possibilities with this treasure!

Sandell, Lisa Ann. *Song of the Sparrow*. **New York: Scholastic, 2007. Ages 11+.**

Poetry; fantasy; romance.

Booktalk: "I am the Lady of Shalott/I come to Camelot/To face all that I fear/To meet all I hold dear." Dear readers, this book describes all my fears and fantasies. Will I marry Lancelot? Will Lancelot favor Gwynivere over me? Will I turn into a witch like King Arthur's sister, Morgan? What is my future?

Note: Written entirely in free-verse poetry, this book can interest girls looking for romance and fantasy. In 490 A.D., 16-year-old Elaine of Ascolat, the Lady of Shalott, has red hair and a temperament to match. She falls in love with the handsome Lancelot and is jealous of Lancelot's love for Gwynivere, King Arthur's wife. This Welsh folktale is legend, taken mainly from Lord Alfred Tennyson's poem "The Lady of Shalott." Includes an author's note and recommended reading.

Smith, Sherri L. *Flygirl*. New York: Putnam, 2008. Ages 9–12.

Historical fiction.

Booktalk: I want to be a pilot. I'm a colored girl. Black girls can't be pilots. So looks like I'm going to have to pass for white. I just hope I can pull it off and become a flygirl!

Note: In World War II (1941–1945), the U.S. government recruited women pilots to fly on non-combat missions. However, no African American women were allowed in the Women Airforce Service Pilots (WASP) program. Eighteen-year-old Ida May Jones decides to pass as white to apply to serve as a WASP. This book inspires many discussions on subjects from sex and race discrimination to "Rosie the Recruiter" and World War II. Visit these Web sites for more information: www.wingsacrossamerica.org and www.waspmuseum.org.

Spiegelman, Art. *The Complete Maus: I: A Survivor's Tale: My Father Bleeds History and II: And Here My Troubles Began*. New York: Pantheon, 1986, 1991. Ages 13+.

Graphic novel; nonfiction.

Booktalk: This graphic novel is controversial. Why? It's the true story of the author's parents and their attempt to survive during the Holocaust in World War II. No problem, right? Except all the Jews are drawn as mice, the Nazis as bloodthirsty cats, the Poles as selfish pigs, the French as frogs, and the Americans as dogs. Many people were offended by this stereotyping. Read this and decide for yourself.

Note: This classic graphic novel is simple in form and complex in theme. Many stimulating discussions will develop (in some cases, without resolution). For *Maus* resources on the Web, with reviews, interviews, and links to Holocaust sites, try www.history.ucsb.edu.

Westerfeld, Scott. *Bogus to Bubbly: An Insider's Guide to the World of the Uglies*. New York: Simon Pulse, 2008. Ages 13+.

Nonfiction.

Booktalk: Have you read the series *The Uglies*? Not to worry. *The Uglies* series started when the author had a friend who went to a dentist. Yes, a dentist. The dentist asked that they develop a five-year plan for his teeth. The author thought this was hilarious. Then all these other ideas came to him. This is the story behind the story of *The Uglies*.

Note: This behind-the-scenes book is a good way to introduce readers to *The Uglies* series, as well as to help them learn the process of writing. Discussions about science, inventions, and the importance of physical appearances are timely and ongoing. Check out the author's innovative Web site and blog at www.scottwesterfeld.com.

CHAPTER 7

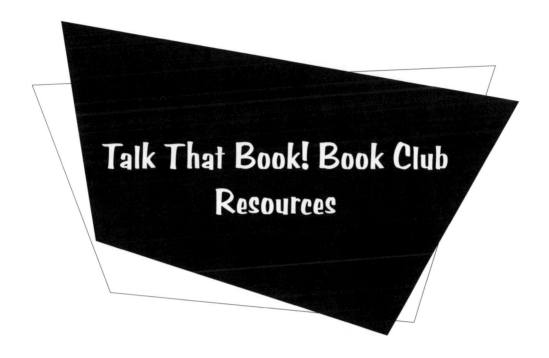

Talk That Book! Book Club Resources

The resources about book clubs listed here provide information about how to begin a book club and offer book lists of recommended group-reads. This chapter provides media recommendations for resources for book clubs and reading research.

American Library Service to Children. *American Library Association*. Web. 1 June 2010.
ALSC provides exceptional Web sites for children and annual Notable Children's Books.

Bookmarks Magazine: For Everyone Who Hasn't Read Everything. Langhorne, PA: Bookmarks. Jon Phillips, publisher and editor. Print.
Consider subscribing to this magazine for all the latest popular reading. However, although children's authors are mentioned, most recommended books refer to adult reading.

"Choices Booklists." *International Reading Association*. Web. 13 Nov. 2009.
Provides lists of titles and authors of annual Choice selections: Children's Choices, Teachers' Choices, and Young Adult Choices.

Daniels, Harvey. *Literature Circles: Voice and Choice in Book Clubs and Reading Groups*. 2nd ed. Portland, ME: Stenhouse, 2002. Print.
This book has been recommended in other chapters, but it is included here because Appendix C contains "Book Lists: Literature Circle Favorites."

Eccleshare, Julia, ed. *1001 Children's Books You Must Read before You Grow Up*. New York: Universe, 2009. Print.

Useful resource for selecting the perfect read, or you may have students choose one of the classics to booktalk. Either way, this beautifully illustrated book is a gem in any collection.

Ellington, Elizabeth, and Jane Freimiller. *A Year of Reading: A Month-by-Month Guide to Classics and Crowd-Pleasers for You or Your Book Group*. Naperville, IL: Source-books, 2002. Print.

A month-by-month guide to reading the best adult (and young-adult) classics. Each month the authors offer five books for the month's read. (In October, try to choose just one of these selections: *The Haunting of Hill House* by Shirley Jackson, *Frankenstein* by Mary Shelley, *On Writing* by Stephen King, *Lives of the Monster Dogs* by Kristen Bakis, or *Neverwhere* by Neil Gaiman.) For each selected book, the guide includes discussions of the book's theme, information about the author, and related Web sites and video resources.

Freeman, Judy. *Stories Kids Will Sit Still For: A Guide to Using Children's Literature, for Librarians, Teachers and Parents,* Vols. 1–3. Fort Atkinson, WI: Upstart, 1984. Print.

Provides multiple resources and reading activities for children. Highly recommended.

Gelman, Judy, and Vicki Levy Krupp. *The Kids' Book Club Book: Reading Ideas, Recipes, Activities, and Smart Tips for Organizing Terrific Kids' Book Clubs*. New York: Penguin, 2007. Print.

Want to know how to run a successful book club? By serving food, of course! Along with the recipes are activities for each selected book. Divided by grades 1–12.

Greenwood, Monique, Lynda Johnson, and Tracy Mitchell-Brown. *The Go On Girl! Book Club Guide for Reading Groups*. New York: Hyperion, 1999. Print.

Begun in 1999 as an informal get-together, this book club is the longest-running reading group for African American adults. Selections include Zora Neal Hurston's *Dust Tracks on a Road* and Gloria Naylor's *The Men of Brewster Place*.

Hahn, Daniel, and Leonie Flynn, eds. *The Ultimate Teen Book Guide*. New York: Walker, 2008. Print.

Recommends more than 700 young adult books and contains sidebars with useful activities.

Hamilton, Emma Walton. *Raising Bookworms: Getting Kids Reading for Pleasure and Empowerment*. Sag Harbor, NY: Beech Tree, 2009. Print.

Book lists and reading motivation techniques for parents, teachers, or any group that uses literature with children.

"Online Book Clubs and Web-based Book Discussion." *Book-Clubs-Resource.com*. Web. 4 June 2010.

Useful mainly for adults, the site provides a list of the best Web sites for book and literary discussion.

"Resources for Book Clubs, Classes and Reading Research." *About.com*. Web. 31 May 2009.

Provides multiple Web sites on book clubs and reading research.

Trelease, Jim. *The Read-Aloud Handbook*. 6th ed. New York: Penguin, 2006. Print.

> Stresses the importance of reading aloud to babies, children, preteens, and teens. Includes helpful book lists and reading research. A weekly read-aloud is available at www.trelease-on-reading.com.

Young Adult Library Service Association. *American Library Association*. Web. 23 Sept. 2009.

> YALSA lists annual book awards and booklists for young adults, including graphic novels, paperbacks, and audiobooks.

Dewey number. Check 374.22 for book clubs or reading groups.

Keyword search. For current information, search "online book clubs," "online book clubs kids," and "online book clubs young adults."

Appendices: Reproducible
Forms

"Battle of the Books" Timeline

DATE OF "BATTLE" _____

Nine to six months ahead:

❑ Receive permission from administration.

❑ Select a date and location for "Battle of the Books," allowing at least three hours.

❑ Plan with community of teachers and librarians.

❑ Select the adult sponsors (timekeeper, scorers, question writers).

❑ Choose and order multiple copies of high-interest books for "Battle of the Books."

❑ Begin reading the selected books.

❑ If required, write easy and difficult questions for each book, noting the page number.

Six to three months ahead:

❑ Allow teams of four (or more) to sign into reading teams.

❑ Supply students with multiple copies of the selected books.

❑ If required, ensure that each team has one adult sponsor.

❑ If required, conduct an orientation for adult sponsors, using some "practice questions."

Two months to one month ahead:

❑ Rehearse with teams using "practice questions."

❑ Begin saving at least three questions—easy, difficult, tiebreaker—for each book at the "Battle."

❑ If prizes are awarded, select the prizes.

❑ If possible, write or find a survey to evaluate the "Battle."

❑ Write publicity announcements and agenda for "Battle of the Books."

One week ahead:

❑ Publicize the event in newspapers, school announcements, local Web sites.

❑ Remind the students and sponsors of the upcoming "Battle."

❑ Prepare arrangements for any refreshments. (Volunteers can provide food.)

One day ahead:

❑ Announce the meeting in the school announcements.

❑ Bring props (e.g., timer, pens, index cards, bell).

❑ Set up and test audiovisual equipment, bringing replacement batteries.

- ❑ Check the environment for safety and comfort.
- ❑ Prepare seating for each team, supplying each team with index cards and black permanent markers.
- ❑ Telephone the volunteers to remind them of time and location.
- ❑ If prizes are awarded, have the prizes available.

On the day:
- ❑ Set up refreshments.
- ❑ Double-check any audiovisual equipment.
- ❑ Begin the "Battle" at the arranged time.
- ❑ If available, provide a survey at the end of the "Battle."

After the "Battle"
- ❑ Write thank-you notes to volunteers.
- ❑ Evaluate the survey to correct any deficiencies.
- ❑ If the "Battle" was successful, plan for the next year!

Notes, including contact information:

_____

_____

_____

_____

_____

_____

_____

_____

_____

_____

Book Club Permission Slip

To parents and guardian, please note the permission slip at the bottom of this page, since this requires your signature.

WHO? Any student interested in reading and reading activities

WHAT? A fun time of eating snacks, discussing books, and creating reading projects

WHERE?

WHEN?

HOW? Just show up at our first meeting with your permission slip!

SPONSOR:

CONTACT INFORMATION:

_____

_____

_____

✂ -

BOOK CLUB PERMISSION SLIP

I give permission for my child to join the Book Club sponsored by _____.

Each meeting will be held on _____

At _____.

Student's name: _____

Parent's name (print): _____

Phone number _____ Emergency phone #: _____

Parent's e-mail address: _____

Parent's signature: _____

If necessary, I will provide transportation before or after the Book Club meetings.

Guest Speaker Checklist

DATE: _____

Two to six months in advance

- ❑ Determine budget, dates, and location.
- ❑ Contact speaker with available dates and costs.
- ❑ If necessary, contact publisher or agent.
- ❑ If necessary, raise funds.

One month in advance

- ❑ Contact libraries, community centers, and schools to advertise the event.
- ❑ Check and repair any equipment that will be used.
- ❑ Write a press release for upcoming event, noting deadlines for submission.

One week in advance

- ❑ Write guest's introduction (short and enthusiastic).
- ❑ Public relations: contact local newspapers, public libraries, and schools.

Day before event

- ❑ Check environment for comfort and safety.
- ❑ Test audiovisual equipment, and set it up. Bring replacement batteries.
- ❑ Contact speaker to confirm date and time.

Day of event

- ❑ Greet author or speaker.
- ❑ Introduce guest.
- ❑ If required, pay guest speaker.
- ❑ Distribute any follow-up survey to the group.

One week after event

- ❑ Write thank-you notes.
- ❑ Read and evaluate comments.
- ❑ Complete any financial records and reports.

Notes, including contact names:

_____

_____

Permission Form for Field Trips

Print copies for students who will be participating in an off-site activity.

School district information: _____

Sponsor's name, phone number, and e-mail:

_____.

The _____ club/group/team has scheduled a field trip on

(date) _____ for (purpose) _____

_____.

The group will leave at (time)_____ and will return at (time)_____.

The cost is $ _____. Lunch arrangements are _____.

Students will travel by transportation in the following form (bus, car, other): _____

_____.

This field trip has been carefully planned and will be conducted under adult supervision.

It is necessary that we have your permission for your child to participate in this educational trip. If you approve, please complete the permission form below. Detach the bottom portion and have your child return it by (date) _____.

_____**Teacher/Sponsor signature**

✂ --

Return to Teacher/Sponsor

FIELD TRIP PERMISSION

My permission is hereby given for my child (name) _____

To attend the field trip with the (group) _____

To (destination) _____.

Under the supervision of _____ on (date) _____.

_____   _____

Print Parent/Guardian Name   Parent/Guardian Signature

I am also interested in being a chaperone:

Address _____

Home Phone number _____

E-mail _____

Publishing Permission Form

DATE: _____

Dear Parents or Guardian,

Our book club is writing, drawing, and creating many reading projects. Some projects will be placed on display in the _____ at _____

_____.

Your child has contributed this project:

The book club is requesting an adult signature so that your child's project will belong to _____

_____.

This project may be displayed and used again and again, in order to motivate other students to read, read, read!

Sponsor: _____

Contact Information: _____

Please sign and return this form:

Student's name: _____

Parent's name (print): _____

Phone number _____ Emergency phone number _____

Parent's e-mail address: _____

Parent's signature: _____

Reader's Profile (Ages 9+)

What is your favorite book? _____

What is your favorite series? _____

Who is your favorite author? _____

What book formats do you like to read? (Circle as many as you want)

Hardbacks

Paperback books

Books on tape/CD/online

Manga/graphic novels/comic books

Magazines

What genres do you prefer? (Circle as many as you want)

Mystery

Horror

Fantasy

Science fiction

Historical fiction

Romance

Sports

Poetry

Fiction (general)

Nonfiction (general)

Biography. What kind of biographies? _____

List any other favorite subject _____

What would you like to do in this book club? (Circle as many as you want)

Arts and crafts

Author visit

Battle of the Books (reading teams compete on the day of the Battle)

Book exchange (exchange books)

Book trailers (create digital booktalks)

Creative dramatics (perform spontaneous skits)

Field trips

Guest speakers

Mystery games (solve mysteries with the group)

One-minute booktalks (talk about a favorite book for 60 seconds)

Poster contest

Puppet show

Rapping rhymes (write or perform a hip-hop rap)

Reader's Theater (read scripts while seated)

Reading games (read books and complete the game)

ScrapBooking (create graphic journals of favorite books)

Soap Opera (write and perform a school soap opera)

Storytelling

Talent Show

Trial by Jury (decide the guilt or innocence of an infamous person)

Young Authors and Illustrators (write or draw)

What do you want to be our first activity?

_____

_____

What other things can we do in the book club?

_____

_____

Check one: Male _____ Female _____

Grade _____ Age _____

Date _____

Author Index of Booktalks

Title Index of Booktalks

Reading Activities by Grade and Age